OCCASIONAL PAPER **226**

Hong Kong SAR:
Meeting the Challenges of Integration with the Mainland

Edited by Eswar Prasad, with contributions from Jorge Chan-Lau, Dora Iakova, William Lee, Hong Liang, Ida Liu, Papa N'Diaye, and Tao Wang

INTERNATIONAL MONETARY FUND
Washington, DC
2004

© 2004 International Monetary Fund

Production: IMF Multimedia Services Division
Composition: Choon Lee
Figures: Theodore F. Peters, Jr.

Cataloging-in-Publication Data

Hong Kong SAR : meeting the challenges of integration with the mainland /
    edited by Eswar Prasad, with contributions from Jorge Chan-Lau . . .
    [et al.]—Washington, D.C.: International Monetary Fund, 2004.

        p. ; cm. — (Occasional paper / International Monetary Fund; 226)

    ISBN 1-58906-294-9

    Includes bibliographical references.

    1. Hong Kong (China) — Foreign economic relations. 2. Fiscal Policy —
China — Hong Kong. 3. Deflation (Finance) — China — Hong Kong.
4. Wages — China — Hong Kong. I. Prasad, Eswar. II. Chan-Lau, Jorge.
III. Series: Occasional paper (International Monetary Fund); no. 226

HF1607.H65 2004

Price: US$25.00
(US$22.00 to full-time faculty members and
students at universities and colleges)

Please send orders to:
International Monetary Fund, Publications Services
700 19th Street, N.W., Washington, D.C. 20431, U.S.A.
Tel.: (202) 623-7430   Telefax: (202) 623-7201
E-mail: publications@imf.org
Internet: http://www.imf.org

recycled paper

Contents

Appendix Table

Figures

The following symbols have been used throughout this paper:

. . . to indicate that data are not available;

— to indicate that the figure is zero or less than half the final digit shown, or that the item does not exist;

– between years or months (e.g., 1998–99 or January–June) to indicate the years or months covered, including the beginning and ending years or months; and

/ between years (e.g., 1998/99) to indicate a fiscal (financial) year.

"Billion" means a thousand million.

Minor discrepancies between constituent figures and totals are due to rounding.

The term "country," as used in this paper, does not in all cases refer to a territorial entity that is a state as understood by international law and practice; the term also covers some territorial entities that are not states, but for which statistical data are maintained and provided internationally on a separate and independent basis.

Preface

This Occasional Paper provides an overview of analytical work done by IMF staff as background for the 2002 and 2003 Article IV consultations with Hong Kong SAR. The paper also draws upon the IMF's recent Financial Sector Stability Assessment (FSSA) of Hong Kong SAR.

The analysis in this paper is based on data available as of July 2003. More recent data do not alter the thrust of the analysis.

The authors would like to express their deep appreciation for the valuable guidance provided by Wanda Tseng and Markus H. Rodlauer. The Hong Kong SAR authorities have been generous in providing data and other information for these studies. The authors are also grateful to the authorities for the extensive discussions and comments that have sharpened the analysis and presentation in this paper. Ioana Hussiada and Song-Yi Kim provided research assistance for this project; Yuko Kobayashi handled the preparation of the manuscript; and Paul Gleason copyedited the paper and coordinated its production and publication.

The opinions expressed in this paper are solely those of its authors and do not necessarily reflect the views of the International Monetary Fund, its Executive Directors, or the Hong Kong SAR authorities.

I Overview

Hong Liang and Eswar Prasad

Hong Kong, Special Administrative Region (Hong Kong SAR) enjoyed impressive economic growth, high levels of income, and close-to-full employment for years until the Asian crisis of 1997 brought about the most severe recession in a generation. Following this, the economy rebounded in 1999 and 2000. Before sustained growth could take hold, however, the global slowdown in 2001 brought on another recession. After four quarters of negative or near-zero growth, the economy of Hong Kong SAR began to show signs of a pickup in the second half of 2002, although domestic demand remained weak. The outbreak of Severe Acute Respiratory Syndrome (SARS) disrupted economic activity once again in the second quarter of 2003. With the rapid containment of SARS, however, there are good prospects of a rebound in activity, supported by strengthening domestic demand and rising exports.

Hong Kong SAR's efforts to cope with the cyclical shocks to its economy have complicated its efforts to undertake the structural adjustments necessitated by its growing integration with the mainland of the People's Republic of China (hereinafter referred to as the mainland). As a small, open economy, Hong Kong SAR's economic performance has been closely tied to changes in the world economy and especially in neighboring countries. By successfully seizing the opportunities provided by the opening up of the mainland, Hong Kong SAR was able to establish itself as the bridge between the mainland and the rest of the world. Since the 1980s, the economic links between Hong Kong SAR and the mainland have expanded rapidly, with Hong Kong SAR becoming the most important trade and international fund-raising center for the mainland. At the same time, Hong Kong SAR has successfully transformed itself into a service-oriented economy as its manufacturing sector has largely relocated to the mainland. Looking forward, rapid economic growth and increased trade between the mainland and the rest of the world should benefit Hong Kong SAR and support the vibrancy of its financial services, logistics, and tourism sectors.

Increasing integration with the mainland has, however, proven to be a double-edged sword, since it has promoted price convergence, exerting downward pressures on goods and factor prices in Hong Kong SAR under the linked exchange rate system. Moreover, the rapid improvement in its neighbors' competitiveness has posed increasing challenges to Hong Kong SAR's traditional advantages and position: its role as a traditional trade intermediary is likely to diminish further as the mainland's trade restrictions are lifted; direct trade relations are established between Taiwan Province of China and the mainland; and more foreign businesses are set up directly on the mainland. Section II, "Economic Integration Between Hong Kong SAR and Mainland China," provides an overview of various dimensions of the economic and financial integration between Hong Kong SAR and the mainland, and the outlook for the further integration of these economies. The analysis points to the significant challenges associated with the process of structural adjustment and the policy implications for Hong Kong SAR. To meet these challenges, Hong Kong SAR's traditional strengths—flexible markets and strong legal and institutional frameworks—will need to be complemented by sound macroeconomic and structural policies.

The recent economic downturn has exposed significant weaknesses in the fiscal structure of Hong Kong SAR. Its revenue system has a narrow base, with a heavy reliance on asset-related revenues, derived mainly from proceeds of land sales and investment incomes. The bursting of the property-price bubble after 1997, coupled with a set of reductions in various fees and charges intended to cushion the impact of the economic slowdown, has driven down the ratio of government revenue to GDP from around 21 percent in fiscal year (FY) 1997 to 14 percent in FY 2002. Meanwhile, government expenditure has grown rapidly in real terms, in part because major spending components, such as civil service salaries and welfare benefits, have not been adjusted for recent deflation. As a result, the consolidated fiscal position has deteriorated gradually since 1998 and substantial structural deficits have emerged. Section III, "Fiscal Outlook and Policy Options," examines how revenues and expenditures might evolve in the medium term in Hong Kong SAR under different policy scenarios and discusses alternative policy options to restore fiscal balance. It argues that the medium-term fiscal consolidation program under way in Hong Kong SAR has to strike a balance between the need to provide comprehensive social services to its citizens and its tradition of limiting the size and role of the government in economic and social affairs.

Developments in the property sector have important implications for the overall economy in Hong Kong SAR. Property prices have been declining steadily since 1997—the peak of the property-price bubble—owing to the weak performance of Hong Kong SAR's economy; overbuilding; and, probably, increased integration with the mainland. Section IV, "Determinants of, and Prospects for, Property Prices," discusses recent developments in the real estate sector and their macroeconomic impact on the economy, and presents estimates and forecasts of fundamental prices in the housing sector. It argues that although property prices now appear to be at levels consistent with demand-side fundamentals, further weakness in housing prices cannot be ruled out if the economy remains weak.

Significant price differentials between Hong Kong SAR and neighboring mainland cities such as Shenzhen and Guangdong, along with the bursting of the property bubble, have been gradually translated into downward pressures on Hong Kong SAR's domestic price level. Deflation has now entered into its fifth successive year. Section V, "Deflation Dynamics," presents a comprehensive econometric analysis of deflation in Hong Kong SAR. It decomposes the aggregate price level into transitory and permanent components, and identifies the nature and origin of the shocks that affect these two components. The analysis shows that although cyclical factors may have triggered the process of deflation, their effects have been perpetuated by the negative wealth and balance-sheet effects in the corporate and household sectors. In addition, price convergence with the mainland has become more important over time in explaining the deflationary process.

Another major challenge posed by increasing integration with the mainland relates to the sectoral reallocation of labor and its impact on income distribution. Until the mid-1990s, Hong Kong SAR's economy was often at or near full employment. This supported strong wage growth, with pay for skilled workers rising particularly quickly. A shift toward higher-value-added services, driven by increased

outsourcing of manufacturing and low-end services to the mainland, has contributed to rising structural unemployment. Section VI, "Trends in Wage Inequality, 1981–2001," examines the evolution of cross-sectional wage inequality in Hong Kong SAR and the impact of structural shifts on wage inequality. The analysis suggests that the most effective policy for addressing rising unemployment and income inequality would be to upgrade the skill level of the labor force.

Over the past two decades, Hong Kong SAR has developed into an important global financial center, spurring the growth of the domestic economy. Financial markets—in particular, the banking system—are well developed, liquid, and efficient. The regulatory infrastructure and supervisory framework have been upgraded continuously to maintain international competitiveness. Section VII, "Financial Market Developments," presents an overview of recent developments in Hong Kong SAR, highlighting new initiatives, such as the introduction of the Securities and Futures Ordinance and a deposit-protection scheme, that are intended to further strengthen the stability of the financial system.

All of the policy issues discussed in this paper are set against the background of the linked exchange rate system (LERS). The LERS, which has been in place since 1983, has served Hong Kong SAR well over the years and remains robust. It has, however, limited the macroeconomic tools available to the government to counter the effects of cyclical shocks and structural shifts. As integration with the mainland deepens and regional competitive pressures continue to intensify, further adjustments in domestic goods and factor prices may be needed. Therefore, prudent fiscal policies, a sound financial system, and improved flexibility of goods and factor markets will be crucial to ensuring the long-term sustainability of the LERS and to enhancing its contributions to economic growth.

Hong Kong SAR has already faced and overcome many challenges. By turning hardship into opportunity, it has built a world-class economy and remains a prominent international financial center. Looking ahead, economic restructuring will—even though it may be painful in the short run—create plenty of new opportunities and a broader scope for development. If it continues to implement a disciplined approach to policymaking that harnesses its fundamental strengths, Hong Kong SAR has a bright and promising future.

II Economic Integration Between Hong Kong SAR and Mainland China

Tao Wang and Hong Liang

Hong Kong SAR's economic ties with the mainland have strengthened since its return to Chinese sovereignty in 1997. Following the relocation of most of its manufacturing production to the mainland in the 1980s and early 1990s, Hong Kong SAR is going through another structural transformation as its economic integration with the mainland deepens in other dimensions. The recently signed Closer Economic Partnership Agreement (CEPA) has provided Hong Kong SAR-based businesses and professionals with access to mainland markets before broader market access to them is provided under China's commitments to the World Trade Organization (WTO). Against this background, this section reviews the process of economic integration between Hong Kong SAR and the mainland, and the policy implications for Hong Kong SAR.

How Much Integration Has Taken Place?

Hong Kong SAR's economic links with the mainland expanded rapidly in the 1980s and the first part of the 1990s, with Hong Kong SAR becoming the most important trade and international fund-raising center for the mainland. Since Hong Kong SAR's return to Chinese sovereignty in 1997, integration between the two economies has deepened: mainland-related entrepôt trade has continued to increase; a large share of China's foreign currency financing is raised in the Hong Kong SAR financial market; a growing range of economic activities are becoming integrated across the border; and business in Hong Kong SAR has increasingly become focused on China-related activities.

Trade

When China began opening up in the late 1970s, Hong Kong SAR's role as an entrepôt was quickly revived, and it became the main intermediary of China's external trade (Cheng and others, 1998). Despite a decline in recent years in the share of China's external trade conducted through Hong Kong SAR, it is still around 40 percent.

As manufacturing activities moved across the border, Hong Kong SAR's economy gravitated toward trade intermediation, and the value of its reexport trade, almost all of which is related to the mainland, is now larger than its GDP. After the mainland opened up, Hong Kong SAR businesses quickly moved their manufacturing bases to southern China while expanding their entrepôt activities. As a result, the share of manufacturing output in Hong Kong SAR's GDP dropped sharply (to 5.2 percent in 2001 from 24.2 percent in 1984), while that of reexports in total exports more than doubled (to 91.6 percent in 2002 from 37.7 percent in 1984). Almost all of Hong Kong SAR's reexports either originate in or are destined for the mainland. The ratio of reexports to GDP has more than tripled since 1984, to 113 percent in 2002.

Entrepôt trade with the mainland and related services are thus critically important to Hong Kong SAR's economy. Total trade—excluding offshore trade—is equivalent to more than 250 percent of GDP, and its contribution to GDP is close to 10 percent (Figure 2.1). In addition, Hong Kong SAR is handling an increasing amount of offshore trade.[1] A survey done in 2001 estimated that the volume of Hong Kong SAR's offshore trade, which has doubled over the past decade, is about the same as that of reexports. More than one in six people employed in Hong Kong SAR are engaged in import and export trading, which contributed some 20 percent to GDP in 2001. This figure does not include trade-related services, such as insurance and financing, sea and air transport, freight forwarding, and advertising and marketing, that, if taken together, would significantly increase the contribution of trade-related activities to GDP.

---

[1]Defined as merchandise trade handled by Hong Kong SAR companies or their subsidiaries but not going through import-export declaration in Hong Kong SAR. It includes both "transshipment" and "offshore trade" as classified in the fifth edition of the IMF's *Balance of Payments Manual*.

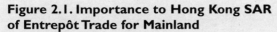

Figure 2.1. Importance to Hong Kong SAR of Entrepôt Trade for Mainland
(*Contribution to Hong Kong SAR's GDP; in percent*)

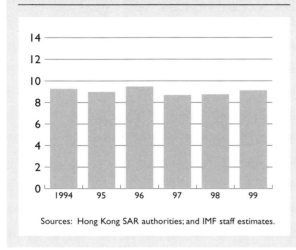

Sources: Hong Kong SAR authorities; and IMF staff estimates.

Finance

Hong Kong SAR has been the most important source of international capital for the mainland. This financing has come in the form of foreign direct investment (FDI), equity and bond financing, and bank lending. (See Section VII for a more detailed discussion of the points noted below.)

- As of 2002, cumulative FDI into the mainland from Hong Kong SAR (from 1979 onward) was estimated at about US$205 billion, or about 45.9 percent of China's total FDI.[2] Although the share of FDI flows from Hong Kong SAR has decreased recently, it still accounted for more than one-third of total FDI flows to the mainland in 2002;
- All but one of the 58 Chinese state-owned enterprises (SOEs) listed abroad at the end of 2001 were listed in Hong Kong SAR, where they had raised a cumulative amount of US$16.6 billion.[3] In 2000, China-related companies (both "red chips" and "H shares") raised a record US$44 billion in the Hong Kong SAR market (Jiang and others, 2001);[4]

- China has raised more than US$4 billion in the Hong Kong SAR bond market (out of $14 billion worth of bonds it has placed outside the mainland) in the last 10 years. Four issues of mainland sovereign bonds were carried out in Hong Kong SAR, and five mainland issues of nongovernment bonds were listed on the Hong Kong SAR exchange at the end of 2002;
- The stock of Hong Kong SAR banks' direct lending to mainland entities totaled some US$37 billion, or about 70 percent of total foreign bank lending to the mainland, in 1999 (IMF, 2000 and 2001).[5] Lending to the mainland by Hong Kong SAR banks has since declined, in part owing to the financial problems of some debtors;[6]
- Hong Kong SAR banks have also been active in arranging syndicated loans and floating-rate notes for use on the mainland. At their peak in 1997, syndicated loans to the mainland arranged by Hong Kong SAR banks totaled US$6.1 billion.

The growing presence of mainland firms and their capital-raising activities has contributed to the development of Hong Kong SAR's financial markets. For instance, the growing number of mainland firms in the equity market has attracted an increasing number of international funds to Hong Kong SAR, which earned good returns: during 1996–2000, the red chip index was up 36 percent, compared with 15 percent for the rest of the market.[7]

Other Business Activities

Hong Kong SAR-funded firms now employ an estimated five million people in China, mostly in manufacturing. Some low-end services, such as retail trade, recreation and leisure, accounting and back-office operations of banks, and some trade-related services, have also started to relocate across the border (CLSA Emerging Markets, 2001). As a

---

[2]Some of the FDI flows may be "round-tripping" from the mainland to take advantage of the preferential treatment of foreign investors in China.

[3]A number of them are also listed in New York.

[4]"H shares" are shares of mainland-incorporated companies listed in Hong Kong SAR, while "red chips" are shares of Hong Kong SAR-incorporated companies with a controlling stake held by state-owned organizations or provincial/municipal authorities on the mainland.

---

[5]Hong Kong SAR banks' direct exposure to the mainland is relatively small, amounting to less than 3 percent of total assets of the banking sector, although their indirect exposure is likely to be higher, since a portion of loans booked for use in Hong Kong SAR are actually used by the borrowers for their mainland operations.

[6]In particular, the problems of international trust and investment corporations (ITICs). The net liabilities of Hong Kong SAR banks to mainland clients have recently increased sharply, largely reflecting the ample liquidity conditions on the mainland and the shrinking exposure of Hong Kong SAR banks to the mainland. There has also been increased lending—although from a very small base—by mainland banks to Hong Kong SAR companies, in part to finance the latter's mainland operations.

[7]Excluding Hong Kong and Shanghai Banking Corporation (a large participant in the market that has seen its share price rise by more than 40 percent during this period).

result, the share of factor income that comes from the mainland has almost tripled, to 23 percent in 2002 from 8 percent in 1995.

As the number of Hong Kong SAR residents visiting Shenzhen and other nearby mainland cities for shopping, entertainment, and leisure has increased, the number of people who live and work on different sides of the border has also increased. Between 1990 and 2002, the number of Hong Kong SAR residents visiting the mainland more than tripled, to 56 million departures (implying that Hong Kong SAR residents averaged eight visits each in 2002). It is estimated that Hong Kong SAR consumers spent HK$19.6 billion in connection with personal travel in Guangdong, equivalent to 11 percent of Hong Kong SAR retail sales, in 2002. Moreover, an estimated 198,100 Hong Kong SAR residents worked on the mainland in 2002, up from 52,300 in 1988.

Mainland's Presence in Hong Kong SAR

The mainland of China has become a major source of FDI for Hong Kong SAR. By the end of 2001, the mainland had invested US$123 billion in Hong Kong SAR (29.3 percent of its total inward FDI). Many firms and government entities have set up offices in Hong Kong SAR to gain international exposure and market opportunities. An estimated 2000 mainland-related companies are currently operating in Hong Kong SAR, with an important presence in the trading, real estate, insurance, transport, finance, and construction sectors. At the end of 2000, 24 branches of mainland banks accounted for 16 percent of total assets and 21 percent of deposits in the Hong Kong SAR banking system (Hong Kong SAR Census and Statistics Department, 2001).

A rising number of visitors from the mainland has helped sustain the Hong Kong SAR tourist industry. In 2001, mainland visitors contributed 37 percent of Hong Kong SAR's tourist receipts, and the number of visitors increased by another 53.4 percent in 2002.

Correlations of Economic and Financial Developments

Hong Kong SAR's economy is increasingly correlated with the mainland's external sector, though not its overall economy. On the one hand, the correlation between Hong Kong SAR's GDP and China's external trade has been strong and has tended to increase in recent years (Figure 2.2).[8] On the other hand, since integration of other sectors is still at an early

_____
[8]Measured by the correlation of estimated deviations from trends over moving subperiods.

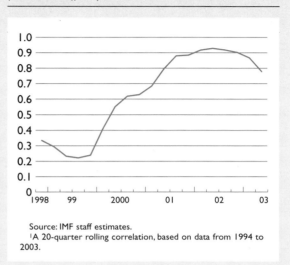

Figure 2.2. Correlation of Hong Kong SAR's GDP and China's Trade Growth[1]
(Correlation coefficient)

Source: IMF staff estimates.
[1]A 20-quarter rolling correlation, based on data from 1994 to 2003.

stage, the correlation of Hong Kong SAR's GDP with the GDP of the mainland has been much weaker.

Despite growing links, the financial markets of Hong Kong SAR and the mainland still remain largely independent of each other. Capital controls, though not watertight, still serve to insulate China's domestic financial market from external developments. In contrast, the linked exchange rate system and absence of any capital controls in Hong Kong SAR have resulted in a high degree of global integration of its financial markets. As a result, correlations between the Hong Kong SAR and mainland financial markets are, on average, weak, although there have been some periods when the correlations have been strongly positive (Figures 2.3 and 2.4).

Outlook for Further Integration with the Mainland

Hong Kong SAR's integration with the mainland will deepen in the coming years, with the mainland economy opening up further following WTO accession (Aziz and others, 2000; and Hong Kong SAR General Chamber of Commerce, 2000). This process is expected to spur additional realignment of output, trade, and investment patterns, and financial flows in the region. In the near term, Hong Kong SAR is likely to benefit from increased trade and investment activities between the mainland and the rest of the world, given the excellent "starting position" that

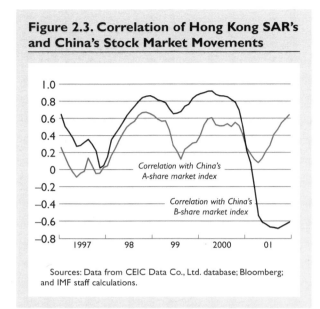

Figure 2.3. Correlation of Hong Kong SAR's and China's Stock Market Movements

Correlation with China's A-share market index

Correlation with China's B-share market index

Sources: Data from CEIC Data Co., Ltd. database; Bloomberg; and IMF staff calculations.

Figure 2.4. Correlation of Hong Kong Dollar and Renminbi Forward Premiums

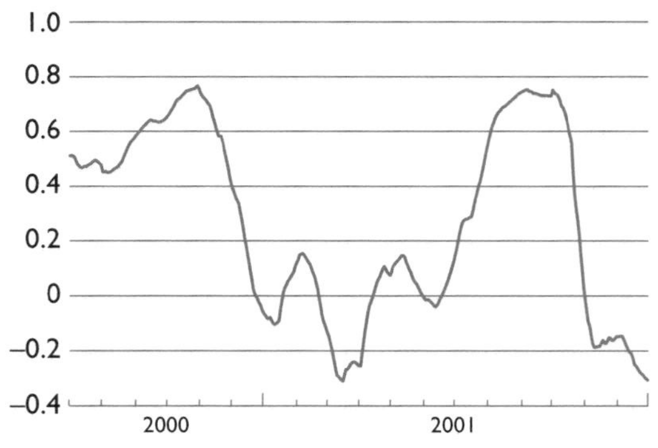

Sources: Bloomberg; and IMF staff calculations.

Hong Kong SAR companies have in intermediating those activities. The zero-import-tariff preference and the WTO-plus market-liberalization measures for trade in services would give companies in Hong Kong SAR a further advantage. In the longer run, however, Hong Kong SAR's traditional role as a middleman will likely diminish, with sources of growth shifting increasingly to higher-value-added service sectors.

Trade

In the next few years, Hong Kong SAR will benefit from increased trade between the mainland and the rest of the world. Even after two decades of rapid growth, China's exports still account for only about 5 percent of world exports. Given China's large labor supply and cost competitiveness, as well as its rising domestic demand, significant scope remains for continued strong expansion of China's trade. (See Rumbaugh and Blancher, 2004.)

Hong Kong SAR's efficient port facilities, trading experience, global logistics network, and agglomeration of trading activities will be hard to rival in the near future. Hong Kong SAR is endowed with a natural deepwater, silt-free harbor, strategically located on major sea routes and with China's export growth engine, the Pearl River delta, as its hinterland. Nearby ports of the mainland do not yet pose a serious challenge; rather, the about twenty small-to-medium-sized ports in the region could complement Hong Kong SAR's port services, helping to lower their overall costs. Hong Kong SAR also has the advantage of major port agglomeration with exten-

sive port and freight-management experience, permitting it to provide complete services, including insurance and finance. A new terminal (to be phased in beginning in 2003) will add significant capacity, providing a solid basis for handling additional trade with China.

Nonetheless, mainland port facilities are improving, and the economy of the Yangtze River basin is gaining in importance. Ports in southern China have expanded rapidly, and mainland exports handled by Hong Kong SAR companies are increasingly shipped directly from the mainland rather than through Hong Kong SAR.[9] Growing competition will come, especially from Shanghai and its surrounding ports, which are situated in the middle of China's coastline, with easy access to the large economic zone along the Yangtze River. Given its location and large industrial base, the Yangtze River region will likely gain further importance as a major engine of growth and exports (Box 2.1).

As China continues to liberalize trade and investment, direct access between the mainland and the rest of the world will increase, potentially bypassing Hong Kong SAR. Under China's WTO commitments, more Chinese firms will be allowed to engage in direct external trade, distribution, and transportation services. At the same time, restrictions on foreign companies are being reduced or abolished. Although Hong Kong SAR companies are also expected to benefit from such liberalization, they

---

[9]A recent survey by the Trade Development Council shows that such direct shipments doubled between 1994 and 2000.

Box 2.1. Hong Kong SAR and Shanghai: A Comparative Perspective

Hinterland

Narrowly defined, Hong Kong SAR's hinterland is the Pearl River delta; more broadly, it could be viewed to include the whole of Guangdong province. Shanghai's hinterland is the Yangtze River delta or, viewed more broadly, may include Jiangsu and Zhejiang provinces. Guangdong province has been the main export engine of China, but Jiangsu and Zhejiang have the potential to catch up, given their large populations and industrial bases and vibrant nonstate sectors. Moreover, goods from other provinces along the Yangtze River could easily reach Shanghai via the river and its extensive branch network. This area would include much of Anhui, Hubei, and Hunan provinces, which have a total population of 285 million.

Comparison of Ports, 2000

Port	Cargo Volume (millions of tons)	Container Traffic (million TEUs)[1]	New Construction	Hinterland
Hong Kong SAR	175, of which 69 percent containerized	18.1, busiest in the world	Terminal 9 will add 2.6 million TEUs capacity	Pearl River delta
Shanghai	204, largest port in China. 25 percent growth per annum in past 10 years	5.6	Deep-sea port being built on outskirt island	Yangtze River delta

Sources: China, Ministry of Communication; and IMF staff estimates.
[1]TEUs= 20-foot equivalent units.

Comparison of Guangdong and Jiangsu Plus Zhejiang, 2001
(In percent of mainland total, unless otherwise noted)

	Guangdong	Jiangsu Plus Zhejiang
GDP	11.1	16.9
Exports	36.0	20.2
Population	6.1	9.4
People with college degree or higher education (millions)	1.5	2.1
Industrial production	14.7	20.6
Share of non-state-owned enterprises in total number of industrial enterprises of region	86.5	91.7

Source: China Statistical Yearbook 2000.

will face intensified competition from both mainland and foreign firms.

Hong Kong SAR's traditional role as a middleman for mainland trade is therefore likely to diminish over time. Reexports are likely to increasingly shift to offshore trade (Table 2.1) or bypass the Hong Kong SAR connection altogether. Although the initial increase in the mainland's overall trade will likely dominate the trade-diversion effects, Hong Kong SAR will eventually have to reduce its reliance on entrepôt trade for the mainland.

Financial Services[10]

With the mainland opening up its financial sector, some foreign financial institutions are likely to relocate their China-related activities from Hong Kong SAR to the mainland, especially Shanghai. Lower business costs and proximity to business and clients

---

[10]Section VII contains a discussion of other aspects of financial integration between Hong Kong SAR and the mainland, and the associated supervisory and regulatory challenges.

Table 2.1. Survey of Traders on Prospects of Different Shipping Arrangements for China Trade
(Views expressed, percentages of total)

	Growth	No Change	Decline
Reexports	18.5	32.5	49.1
Transshipments via			
Hong Kong SAR	37.2	36.8	26.0
Direct shipment	76.7	17.9	5.4

Source: Hong Kong SAR, Trade Development Council.

would be the main attractions of moving to the mainland. Shanghai is an industrial and commercial center where many foreign production facilities are located, and it has an ample supply of relatively well-educated labor. In addition, the government has continued to invest heavily in Shanghai's infrastructure, and the city is gaining expertise as a financial center.

Nonetheless, Hong Kong SAR has advantages that will likely preserve its role as a center for China's international capital-raising activities for the foreseeable future:

- A sound legal framework and an independent and efficient judiciary;
- Free flow of capital and information; and
- A mature financial market and sound banking system.

These factors will make it difficult for Shanghai or other cities on the mainland to rival Hong Kong SAR as a major international financial center in the near future.

Growing financing needs on the mainland will likely benefit Hong Kong SAR in its role as an international financial center. Given China's high saving rate, much of the financing needed for the expansion of domestic investment will be raised domestically. Nonetheless, a significant part will be raised abroad, and Hong Kong SAR—with its well-developed market infrastructure and experience—could benefit in the following areas:

- Increasing placements by large Chinese state-owned enterprises and private firms in the Hong Kong SAR stock market;
- Restructuring and infrastructure projects on the mainland should help boost Hong Kong SAR's debt market (A 1996 World Bank report estimated that China's infrastructure-related spending could exceed US$700 billion over 10 years, and preparation for the 2008 Olympics may require additional infrastructure spending.);

- Growing corporate debt financing by mainland firms (If China's corporate debt-to-GDP ratio were to reach 4 percent—the level in Thailand before the crisis—by 2010, corporate bonds outstanding could total more than $120 billion, compared with the current $10 billion.);
- FDI flows to China will likely increase with WTO-related liberalization of the services sector and the elimination of textile export quotas in 2005. Some of this FDI is likely to continue to be channeled through Hong Kong SAR.

Hong Kong SAR firms could benefit from the opening up of China's financial sector, although they will face competition from international firms. Under China's WTO commitments, mainland banking, insurance, and asset-management industries will gradually open up to foreign firms. The Closer Economic Partnership Agreement (CEPA) between Hong Kong SAR and the mainland, which went into effect on January 1, 2003, will give Hong Kong SAR firms access to these sectors two years before foreign firms and with lower entrance requirements. Hong Kong SAR firms could potentially benefit from this liberalization, given their extensive experience in these areas. However, Hong Kong SAR firms will eventually have to compete with much larger and well-established international firms.

Business Services

Migration of certain trade-related services to the mainland is likely to continue. A survey by Hong Kong SAR's Trade Development Council indicates that more than three-fourths of Chinese exports handled by Hong Kong SAR now have freight forwarding and consolidation arranged on the mainland, and over half of the testing and certification is also conducted there. As China opens up its services sector further, this trend is likely to continue.

Nevertheless, although some foreign companies may relocate to the mainland, Hong Kong SAR is still very attractive as a business center. As foreign businesses' presence on the mainland expands, cheaper labor and office space may induce regional offices and China-related operations to move from Hong Kong SAR across the border. Hong Kong SAR could gradually lose its predominance as a center for China-related foreign businesses. Hong Kong SAR, however, still has many advantages (described in Section III) that seem to justify a significant cost premium. The number of regional headquarters and offices in Hong Kong SAR increased by 24 percent between 1997 and 2002, to over 3,000 (Table 2.2), and the presence of Chinese firms, which declined during 1998–99, has started to grow again.

The Hong Kong SAR tourism industry, although still relatively small, could be an important source of

Table 2.2. Hong Kong SAR as a Regional Headquarters for Multinational Companies

	1997	1998	1999	2000	2001	2002
Number of regional headquarters and offices in Hong Kong SAR	2,514	2,449	2,490	3,001	3,237	3,119
Of which: those with parent companies incorporated on the mainland	243	205	205	229	242	266
Number of persons engaged in regional headquarters and offices in Hong Kong SAR *(in thousands)*[1]	...	136	114	133	173	165
Of which: those with parent companies incorporated on the mainland	...	7.6	7.3	9.2	7.2	6.6

Source: Hong Kong SAR, Census and Statistics Department.
[1]Excluding those who did not respond.

growth in the future. Tourism receipts were equivalent to 4.9 percent of its GDP in 2001, with 37 percent coming from mainland Chinese visitors. Further relaxation of restrictions on visas/quotas for mainland visitors to Hong Kong SAR could boost tourism significantly in the coming years.

Challenges of Integration

To meet the challenges of integration, Hong Kong SAR must continue to enhance its competitive advantage and attract higher-value-added business activities. As an advanced, relatively high-wage economy, Hong Kong SAR cannot compete with the mainland in activities such as labor-intensive manufacturing and low-end services. It will have to "move up the value chain," following the examples of some companies that have successfully adjusted their business structures (Box 2.2). As noted, China's growth, increasing financing needs, and further liberalization offer great opportunities for Hong Kong SAR—with such a vast and vibrant hinterland, Hong Kong SAR can further develop what it does best and consolidate its role as a major international financial, trade, and business center.

A recent survey on trade and trade-related services shows that many Hong Kong SAR companies are planning to change their business operations along these lines. Table 2.3 shows that companies plan to move lower-value-added trade-related services to the mainland while focusing Hong Kong SAR operations on higher-value-added activities.

To take full advantage of this structural shift, Hong Kong SAR will need to further enhance its comparative advantage. A survey of foreign companies with regional representation in Hong Kong SAR identified the following major advantages that it possesses (in decreasing order of importance): (1) low tax rates and a simple tax system; (2) free flow of information; (3) political stability and security;

(4) corruption-free government; (5) up-to-date communications, transport, and other infrastructure; (6) rule of law and independent judiciary; (7) business-friendly government economic policy; (8) absence of exchange controls; (9) free-port status; and (10) level playing field.

The structural changes resulting from integration could lead to higher structural unemployment and a shortage of skilled workers. A recent study by the Hong Kong Monetary Authority (Peng, Cheung, and Fan, 2001) finds that the natural rate of unemployment has risen modestly in recent years, and there is evidence of an increased skills mismatch in the ser-

Table 2.3. Location of Major Operations of Hong Kong SAR Companies in Next Five Years
(Business location, in percent of total respondents)

	Hong Kong SAR	Mainland China	Other
Trade financing/documentation	90.1	16.1	4.4
Regional headquarters/offices	85.4	18.8	5.0
Insurance	84.9	19.5	6.9
Business negotiation	72.4	39.7	18.5
Arbitration	71.5	35.0	9.6
Marketing	58.1	37.6	30.5
Freight forwarding and consolidation	55.3	58.5	9.0
Production development/design	53.4	46.6	16.2
Testing/certification	46.2	59.1	12.0
Material sourcing	38.3	71.9	20.2
Warehousing/inventory control	30.6	77.8	5.9
Sample making/prototyping	27.2	73.4	11.0
Quality control	25.9	78.0	10.5
Manufacturing/packaging	14.4	86.3	10.8

Source: Hong Kong SAR, Trade Development Council.

Box 2.2. "Moving Up the Value Chain": An Example

The evolution of Li & Fung Limited, one of the world's leading trading companies of consumer products, provides an example of how Hong Kong SAR companies are adjusting to the effects of rising integration with the mainland.

As manufacturing moved from Hong Kong SAR to the mainland in the 1980s, the company shifted its sourcing from local manufacturers to the mainland while focusing its Hong Kong business on supply-chain management. Today, the company uses its experience and global network to provide a complete services package including product development, raw-material sourcing, production planning and management, quality assurance, and shipping. For example, when a client orders a line of leather jackets, the company can arrange to have the leather acquired from India, have it tanned in the Republic of Korea, buy plated metal buckles from Japan, do cutting and sewing in China, and export the finished jackets from China. Interactive services ensure that the client can change the order—in terms of quantity, color, and cut—even at a relatively advanced stage of the production process.

Taking advantage of Hong Kong SAR's location, openness, complete range of supporting services (finan-cial, legal, transport), simple tax system, and valuable human capital, the company manages its sales and marketing, contract negotiation, control, and information flow from its Hong Kong SAR headquarters. At the same time, activities closer to manufacturing—such as molding and engineering, testing and quality control, and storage and shipment of cargo—have been moved closer to the factory floor on the mainland of China and elsewhere.

The company has expanded its operations to some forty countries, diversifying its supply sources and markets. This has allowed it to serve clients at a low cost and rapidly, and to reduce reliance on any one country. Modern telecommunications have enabled the company to manage its global business from Hong Kong SAR. For example, instead of on-site inspection of design and production, Li & Fung now mostly relies on digital-camera and Internet transmission. Thus, the company's operations in Hong Kong SAR have continued to grow, even if virtually nothing is sourced from there any longer.

With the further opening up of the mainland, Li & Fung is likely to increase its sourcing from there, and the company views Hong Kong SAR as an ideal location for managing this expansion.

---

vices sector. The government's 2001 manpower projection report estimates that by 2007, Hong Kong SAR will have a shortage of some 99,000 people with higher education and a surplus of about a quarter of a million people with a secondary-school education or less (Table 2.4).

These labor-market pressures will continue to challenge education and other social policies. As is discussed in more detail in Section VI, structural change is the main factor behind the increase in income inequality over the last two decades. To meet the growing demand for highly skilled workers, Hong Kong SAR will have to further strengthen its education and training programs, and may also need to adjust its immigration policies. In this vein, a new Admission for Mainland Talents and Professionals Scheme took effect in July 2003. The scheme aims to attract skilled workers and professionals from the mainland to work in Hong Kong SAR in order to meet local manpower needs and enhance Hong Kong SAR's competitiveness in the global market.

Meeting the challenges of integration will also have fiscal implications. Upgrading the education system, infrastructure development, and higher unemployment could create pressures for higher public expenditures, leading to measures to contain costs and/or obtain offsetting savings elsewhere. At the same time, relocation of more economic activities from Hong Kong SAR to the mainland could result in lower revenues, given the territorial-source principle of income taxation, thereby pointing to the need for measures to strengthen the revenue base.[11]

Table 2.4. Projected Manpower Resource Balance in 2005

Education Attainment	Projected Manpower Resource Balance	
	(persons)	(percentage of supply)
Lower secondary and below	133,500	11.8
Upper secondary	82,500	8.6
Craft	15,600	51.7
Postsecondary	−62,600	−32.9
First degree and above	−36,500	−5.8

Source: Hong Kong SAR government (2003).

---

[11]Hong Kong SAR, Task Force on Review of Public Finances, 2002.

III Fiscal Outlook and Policy Options

Hong Liang

Fiscal policy in Hong Kong SAR has traditionally been conservative. The fiscal balance remained in surplus between FY1985 and FY1997, resulting in an accumulated fiscal reserve of about 35 percent of GDP in FY1997. In addition, fiscal policy had not been used as a countercyclical tool before the Asian crisis.[1]

The fiscal position has gradually deteriorated, however, since FY1998 (Figure 3.1). A cyclical rise in the budget deficit has been combined with a structural weakening of the fiscal position, leading to consolidated deficits of 5 percent of GDP in FY2001 and 5½ percent of GDP in FY2002. In February 2002, the government's Task Force on Public Finances found rising structural deficits in recent years primarily owing to (1) lower revenues from land sales and taxes, (2) falling investment income, and (3) the government expenditure deflator rising faster than the general price level. Its report noted that the operating account had been in deficit since FY1998. Furthermore, without investment income, the operating deficits since FY1998 would have been much larger (Table 3.1). IMF staff estimates also indicate that substantial structural deficits have emerged, increasing from 5½ percent of GDP in FY2001 to 6½ percent in FY2002.[2]

This section aims to
- provide indicative estimates of how revenue and expenditure might evolve over the next five years under two fiscal-consolidation scenarios, each with a different mix of revenue/expenditure measures designed to bring the fiscal position into balance by FY2006;
- examine different revenue-raising measures in light of the findings of the Advisory Committee on New Broad-Based Taxes;

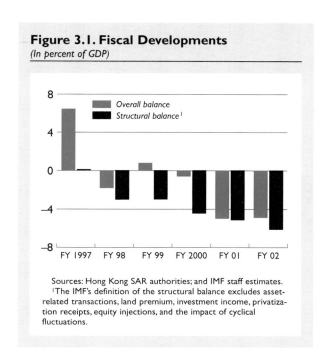

Figure 3.1. Fiscal Developments
(In percent of GDP)

Legend:
- Overall balance
- Structural balance[1]

Sources: Hong Kong SAR authorities; and IMF staff estimates.
[1]The IMF's definition of the structural balance excludes asset-related transactions, land premium, investment income, privatization receipts, equity injections, and the impact of cyclical fluctuations.

- discuss features of major government expenditure components (civil service pay, education, health, and welfare) using comparative perspectives, highlighting their rapid growth in both nominal and real terms in recent years; and
- offer some thoughts on areas where potential expenditure savings could be made.

Medium-Term Fiscal Outlook

The findings of the Task Force on Public Finances illustrate the precarious fiscal situation in Hong Kong SAR in the medium term. The budget model developed by the task force takes into account the prevailing government expenditure and revenue developments, notably that government expenditure has been growing faster than nominal GDP, and the likely impact of the consolidation of the property market and the aging population. The task force con-

---

[1]Note that this analysis is based on data available as of July 2003. Fiscal developments since then do not substantially alter the thrust of the policy analysis in this section.

[2]The structural fiscal balance is used to measure the impact of discretionary fiscal policy on domestic demand. The IMF's definition excludes asset-related transactions, land premiums, investment income, privatization receipts, equity injections, and the impact of cyclical fluctuations.

Table 3.1. Operating Account
(In percent of GDP)

	Fiscal Years											
	1991	1992	1993	1994	1995	1996	1997	1998	1999	2000	2001	2002
Operating balance after investment income	4.2	4.4	4.8	4.0	2.7	2.9	3.3	−0.1	−0.1	−1.2	−3.7	−3.7
Investment income	0.4	0.2	0.4	0.5	0.6	0.4	1.1	2.5	3.0	1.6	0.0	1.3
Operating balance before investment income	3.8	4.2	4.4	3.5	2.1	2.5	2.2	−2.6	−3.1	−2.8	−3.8	−5.0

Source: Hong Kong SAR authorities.

cluded that without corrective measures, continued sizable deficits in the range of 4–5 percent of GDP per annum are probable in the medium term, leading to a depletion of fiscal reserves by FY2008 at the latest, followed by a rising debt burden.[3] In contrast, IMF staff projections indicate that—owing to higher projected deficits in FY2002 and FY2003 than those based on the task force's assumptions—in the absence of specific reform measures, Hong Kong SAR's fiscal reserves could be depleted as early as FY2006. (Figure 3.2).

The government announced, in the FY2002 budget, its intention to return to a balanced budget by FY2006. In the FY2003 budget, it reaffirmed this

---

[3]The portion of fiscal reserves held in foreign currencies is included in the official foreign exchange reserves of Hong Kong SAR.

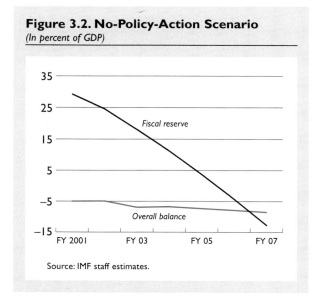

Figure 3.2. No-Policy-Action Scenario
(In percent of GDP)

Source: IMF staff estimates.

objective and proposed to achieve fiscal consolidation using a three-pronged approach based on cutting expenditures, increasing tax rates, and boosting economic growth.

Two scenarios have been developed by the IMF staff to illustrate the implications of choosing a different mix of expenditure and revenue for achieving the targeted fiscal consolidation in the medium term.

Basic Assumptions[4]

- In both scenarios, real GDP growth is assumed to be 1.5 percent in 2003, gradually returning to its potential of 3.5 percent annually over the medium term. Deflation is projected to continue at 2.6 percent in 2003 and to gradually dissipate by FY2006. For FY2003, the revenue and expenditure assumptions are based on the March 2003 budget proposal. The cost of the temporary-relief measures proposed in April 2003 to mitigate the economic impact of SARS is included in the calculation of the fiscal deficit for FY2003 but is not included in deficit projections for subsequent years, given that these were one-time measures.
- On the revenue side, all recurrent revenue items (except investment income) are assumed to grow at the same rate as nominal GDP, and capital revenues (including land premiums) are assumed to be 2.8 percent of nominal GDP annually, in line with their historical averages before the mid-1990s. A nominal rate of return of 5 percent is assumed for investment income on fiscal reserves.

---

[4]The details for the key parameters of the IMF staff's projections are set out in the appendix. It should be noted that the medium-term projections are based on a partial-equilibrium analysis and should be viewed more as illustrations of the plausible future fiscal path than as firm results.

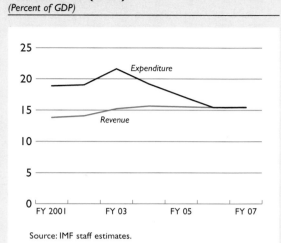

Figure 3.3. Scenario 1: Fiscal Consolidation Path Without Introduction of a Goods and Services Tax (GST)
(Percent of GDP)

Source: IMF staff estimates.

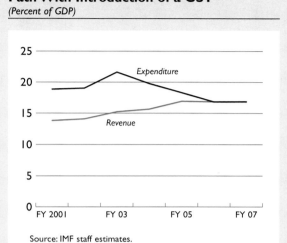

Figure 3.4. Scenario 2: Fiscal Consolidation Path With Introduction of a GST
(Percent of GDP)

Source: IMF staff estimates.

- On the expenditure side, the government expenditure deflator is assumed to grow at the same rate as nominal GDP after FY2006, when a balanced budget is achieved; and social security expenditure is projected to grow in line with the long-term population projections.[5]

Path of Fiscal Consolidation

- Under both scenarios, the fiscal deficit would widen to 6.3 percent of GDP in FY2003, or 1 percent of GDP higher than was proposed in the March budget, on account of the temporary SARS relief package. At the same time, the proposed revenue measures, mainly increases in tax rates on profits and salaries, are expected to yield a total of HK$14 billion in additional revenues over the period FY2003–FY2005 (Figure 3.3).
- In Scenario 1, no further revenue measures are introduced after FY2003. As a result, an expenditure cut (excluding social security expenditure) of 10.5 percent per annum for three years will be needed for Hong Kong SAR to reach a balanced budget by FY2006. This implies a revenue/expenditure-to-GDP ratio of 15 percent in the long run. In this scenario, revenue efforts

provide about 20 percent of the required fiscal adjustment of 5–6 percent of GDP.
- In Scenario 2, a goods and services tax (GST) of 3 percent is assumed to be introduced in FY2005, with a projected revenue yield of 1.4 percent of GDP. Consequently, expenditure (excluding social security expenditure) will need to be cut by only 7.2 percent per annum between FY2004 and FY2006, resulting in an expenditure-to-GDP ratio of 16.8 percent in the long run. In this scenario, revenue efforts contribute about 45 percent of the required fiscal adjustment (Figure 3.4).

The two fiscal-consolidation scenarios illustrate that the share of government expenditures in GDP needs to be adjusted significantly if Hong Kong SAR intends to maintain its tradition of having low taxes. In the absence of significant new revenue measures besides the GST, and assuming the shares of property- and stock-related revenues in GDP return to their pre-1990 levels, the total government expenditure-to-GDP ratio would need to be cut from its current level of nearly 20 percent to 16–17 percent by FY2006 to balance the budget. If a GST were not introduced, the expenditure-to-GDP ratio would need to fall to around 15 percent.

Revenue Structure

Notable features of Hong Kong SAR's revenue structure are (1) the tax burden is low (9 percent of GDP) and the tax system is simple; (2) the tax base

---

[5]The revenue and expenditure parameters are largely drawn from the assumptions in the budget model in the "Final Report of the Task Force on Review of Public Finances," Hong Kong SAR, February 2002.

Table 3.2. Revenue Structure
(In percent of total government revenue, unless otherwise indicated)

	Fiscal Years							
	1995	1996	1997	1998	1999	2000	2001	2002
Taxes	67.0	67.1	56.3	53.3	47.9	56.1	71.2	67.8
Of which:								
Earnings and profits tax	43.0	40.3	32.5	35.0	28.7	32.8	44.3	41.4
Stamp duties	6.2	9.8	10.3	4.7	5.2	4.8	4.9	6.2
Other revenue	33.0	32.9	43.7	46.7	52.1	43.9	28.8	32.2
Of which:								
Land sales and Land Fund revenue	10.4	12.6	24.8	13.6	24.1	18.8	17.8	13.8
Investment income	3.3	2.7	3.2	10.0	6.6	7.3	6.2	...
Sales of government assets	...	...	...	...	...	4.5	0.2	...
Memorandum item:								
Total revenue as percentage of GDP	16.4	17.2	20.9	16.9	18.7	17.5	13.8	14.1

Sources: Hong Kong SAR authorities; and IMF staff estimates.

is narrow, with neither general-consumption taxes nor any import duties, and a majority of the working population is outside the tax net; and (3) nontax revenues, mainly from proceeds of land sales and investment income, generally account for almost half of total revenue (Table 3.2).

Hong Kong SAR's heavy reliance on asset-related revenue makes its revenue system highly volatile and procyclical. Total fiscal revenues averaged 17 percent of GDP between FY1990 and FY2002, with a standard deviation of 2 percent. Land revenue and stamp duties are the most volatile revenue components, and are closely correlated with movements in property and stock prices. Moreover, investment income on the government's asset holdings in the Exchange Fund has become another major contributor to the volatility of fiscal revenues in recent years. Without this investment income, the fiscal deficits since FY1998 would have been much larger.

The Advisory Committee on New Broad-Based Taxes concluded, in its report in 2002, that a low-rated GST would be the best option for Hong Kong SAR to broaden its tax base. A 3 percent GST is estimated to yield around $18 billion (1.4 percent of GDP in 2001) in additional revenue annually. Implementation of a GST in Hong Kong SAR, however, may require two to three years of preparatory work. Administrative preparation will need to cover a wide range of tasks, such as drafting legislation; carrying out consultation, publicity, and education; determining and meeting staffing needs; undertaking training of staff; developing systems, proce-

dures, and forms for collection; and preparing manuals and guidelines.

To compensate for revenue shortfalls pending the implementation of the GST, the advisory committee cited the following interim options: higher income tax rates, lower personal income tax deductions, and a land and sea departure tax. The FY2003 budget set a target of raising revenue by HK$20 billion by FY2006. Measures for raising HK$14 billion in additional revenues, mainly through increases in rates of profits and salaries taxes, have been proposed. The government indicated that other revenue measures would be introduced in the next few years to bring in the additional HK$6 billion needed to achieve the revenue target by FY2006. It has also declared that a GST is essential for broadening the tax base and stabilizing public revenues in the long term. In view of the long lead time required for its implementation, technical preparations for a GST will have to get under way in the near future if it is to make a significant contribution to Hong Kong SAR's medium-term fiscal-consolidation objective.

Government Expenditures

Nominal government expenditures have persistently grown faster than nominal GDP, since prices pertaining to government spending have risen faster than the general price level. This has resulted in an increase in the government expenditure-to-GDP ratio from less than 15 percent in FY1990 to close to

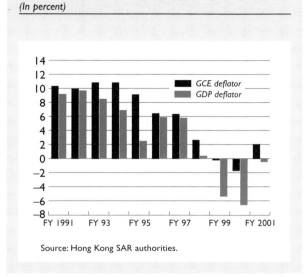

Figure 3.5. Changes in Government Consumption Expenditure (GCE) Deflator and Gross Domestic Product (GDP) Deflator
(In percent)

Source: Hong Kong SAR authorities.

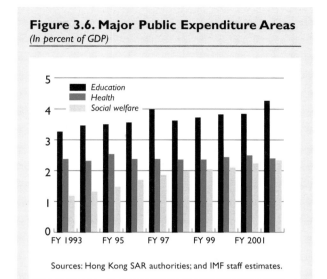

Figure 3.6. Major Public Expenditure Areas
(In percent of GDP)

Sources: Hong Kong SAR authorities; and IMF staff estimates.

20 percent in FY2002.[6] One of the key reasons for the price rigidity of government expenditure is that salaries of civil servants and employees of government-funded organizations, pensions, and social-security payments have not been adjusted downward in nominal terms to account for deflation (Figure 3.5).

Education (21 percent of total public expenditures), health care (12 percent), and welfare (12 percent) are the major areas of public expenditures. Expenditures in all three areas have grown faster in real terms than GDP over the last few years. In particular, welfare spending has more than doubled over the past decade (Figure 3.6).

Given the heavy wage content of government expenditure, it is useful to first examine issues relating to civil-service pay and then discuss developments in the three major expenditure areas. The analysis will incorporate some cross-country comparative perspectives using available data. Two indicators are frequently used to compare subcategory government expenditures internationally: these are subcategory expenditures as a percentage of GDP and as a percentage of total public expenditure. It should be noted that total government expenditure as a percentage of GDP, currently at 20 percent, is very low

by international standards. This reflects the deliberate policy of maintaining a small government in Hong Kong SAR. On average, government expenditures were more than 40 percent of GDP in Organization for Economic Cooperation and Development (OECD) countries in 2001. Therefore, the notion of affordability of a particular public service in Hong Kong SAR should be analyzed within the institutional setting of a small government rather than of a welfare state.

Civil-Service Pay

The civil service in Hong Kong SAR employs about 5 percent of the labor force, with an associated wage bill of 5.5 percent of GDP in FY2001, compared with 4.2 percent of GDP, on average, for high-income countries, as estimated by the World Bank.[7] However, as a percentage of total government expenditure, the civil-service wage bill in Hong Kong SAR—at 30 percent—is almost twice as high as in other high-income countries. In addition, personnel-related expenses account for 70 percent of government operating expenditure. Civil servants account for about half of these expenses, with the rest consisting of payroll expenses for employees of government-funded organizations ("subvented employees"), whose wages are linked to those of civil servants. Aside from salary payments, various benefits and allowances make up a

---

[6]Although the Basic Law of Hong Kong SAR stipulates that the government should keep expenditure growth commensurate with the growth rate of GDP, it does not specify explicitly whether such growth should be measured in nominal or real terms.

[7]See the World Bank's Administrative and Civil Service Reform website (*http://www1.worldbank.org/publicsector/civilservice/*) for cross-country data on government employment and wages.

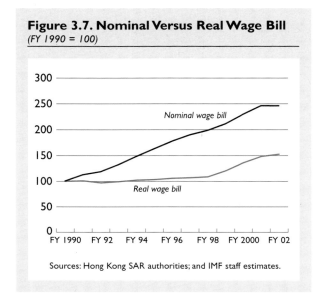

Figure 3.7. Nominal Versus Real Wage Bill
(FY 1990 = 100)

Sources: Hong Kong SAR authorities; and IMF staff estimates.

significant portion of the remuneration package for civil servants.

The civil-service-pay adjustment system has relied heavily on a formula-based mechanism intended to achieve broad comparability with the private sector in Hong Kong SAR. Comparability is often difficult to establish, however, since there is no comparable activity in the private sector for some government activities, such as maintaining a police force. The last pay-level survey was done in 1986, and pay-trend surveys are conducted annually as a basis for annual civil-service-pay adjustment. Nominal wages continue to be adjusted upward even though the overall economy has been experiencing persistent deflation (Figure 3.7).[8] As a result, the wage bill has grown by 11 percent per annum in real terms since FY1998.[9]

Generally, civil-service remuneration packages compare favorably with those in the private sector. The average government-to-private sector wage ratio stood at 3.3 in 2002, compared with an East Asian average of 2.9.[10] However, the economic downturn since 1997 has brought to the forefront the issue of

perceived pay disparities between the civil service and the private sector.[11] Although median earnings (including bonus) for all industries grew at an average rate of 0.8 percent in nominal terms between FY1997 and FY2001, the annual nominal increase in the civil-service wage bill was 6.9 percent during the same period. A pay-level survey conducted in 1999 on starting salaries resulted in the downward adjustment of starting pay of 6–31 percent for the majority of civil-service grades.

To address concerns about the current annual pay-adjustment mechanism, a task force was set up in early 2002 to conduct a comprehensive review of the pay policy and system for the civil service. An analytical study was carried out on the latest developments in civil-service-pay administration in five countries (Australia, Canada, New Zealand, Singapore, and the United Kingdom).[12] Among the study's findings on common trends in pay policy were that affordability within budget constraints has become a dominant consideration, with correspondingly less importance given to formal pay comparability with the private sector. In addition, a clean wage policy consolidating various benefits and allowances with base salaries has been a common feature in the surveyed countries, since it has provided administrative cost savings, reduced opportunities for abuse, and allowed greater spending flexibility for staff.

In its "Phase One Final Report," the task force recommended that (1) in the short run, priority be given to conducting a pay-level survey and adopting appropriate interim measures for annual civil-service-pay adjustment pending the outcome of the pay-level review; and (2) performance pay and flexible pay ranges, decentralization of pay administration, and a clean wage policy be introduced in the medium-to-long term. In February 2003, the government announced its decision to reduce the salaries of civil servants to the level, in cash terms, in effect at the end of June 1997. In addition, the government intends to implement a number of improvements to the pay-adjustment system for the civil service, including completing a new pay-level survey by 2004.

---

[8]The assumption of a 4.75 percent cut in civil-service pay in the FY2002 budget met with strong opposition and was implemented only halfway.

[9]In this section, the government wage bill refers to total government personnel-related expenses. The composite consumer price index (CPI) series is used in this study to derive the real growth rates of various public expenditures to estimate the extent to which public expenditures have grown faster than the overall economy.

[10]This ratio is estimated using median earnings (including bonuses) for all industries and the average salary of a civil servant, derived by dividing the total civil-service wage bill by the number of civil servants.

[11]A study commissioned by the Hong Kong SAR General Chamber of Commerce found in February 2003 that pay for government employees was 17 percent higher than average pay for employees in the business sector. When the cost of benefits is added (even excluding housing and education), the gap widens to 40 percent.

[12]The study was to cover the following five areas: (1) the pay policies, pay system, and pay structure; (2) the experience of replacing fixed pay scales with pay ranges or other pay systems; (3) the pay-adjustment system and mechanism; (4) the experience with introducing performance-based rewards to better motivate staff; and (5) the experience with simplification and decentralization of pay administration.

Table 3.3. Expenditures per Student, by Level of Education, 1999
(In equivalent U.S. dollars converted using PPPs)

	Hong Kong SAR	OECD Average	United States	Korea	Japan
Primary education					
Spending per student *(U.S. dollars)*	2,502	4,148	6,982	2,838	5,240
Ratio of spending per student to GDP per capita *(in percent)*	10	19	20	21	21
Secondary education					
Spending per student *(U.S. dollars)*	4,307	5,465	8,157	3,208	5,612
Ratio of spending per student to GDP per capita *(in percent)*	18	23	24	24	23
Tertiary education					
Spending per student *(U.S. dollars)*	26,161	9,210	19,220	5,356	10,278
Ratio of spending per student to GDP per capita *(in percent)*	108	44	57	39	41

Sources: OECD (2002a); and IMF staff estimates.

Notes: OECD denotes the Organization for Economic Cooperation and Development. PPP denotes purchasing power parity.

Education, Health Care, and Welfare Spending

Education

Education spending, the largest expenditure component in the budget, has grown by more than 7 percent annually in real terms since FY1996, compared with average real GDP growth of about 2.7 percent. The entire education system in Hong Kong SAR, from primary school to university, is basically financed by the government, but each school has considerable flexibility and autonomy in managing its own operations and resources. There is universal attendance from age 6 to 15 (the dropout rate is minimal by international standards), and upper-secondary and tertiary education are highly subsidized.

Hong Kong SAR's pattern of distribution of resources among different levels of education differs considerably from those of other countries (Bray, 1993). In developed countries, resources tend to be more evenly distributed among students at all levels. Although spending per student in higher education is usually more than in primary or secondary schools, the gap is relatively small. The disparity between government spending on higher education and on basic education, however, is significant in Hong Kong SAR. The low level of funding for primary schools is particularly noticeable. Per pupil spending by the government for primary education is about 60 percent of the OECD average (Table 3.3).

Hong Kong SAR allots one-third of its expenditure to tertiary education. Apart from some postsecondary and vocational programs, the enrollment rate for government-funded universities was only 17 percent of the relevant age group in 2001, compared with more than 50 percent in most OECD countries. Some residents have chosen to study abroad, in part owing to the intense competition for places in local institutions of tertiary education. The low enrollment rate for higher education has permitted the government to maintain high-cost institutions and charge low fees. Per student expenditure in government-funded universities was about US$26,000 in 1999, almost two times higher than the OECD average. Students contributed, on average, another US$4,000 a year in fees and charges.

Salaries constitute the largest part of recurrent expenditures on education. More than 80 percent of spending on schools went to recurrent expenditures, which are basically teachers' salaries. Again, the disparity between higher education and primary education is significant.[13] The average remuneration package for college professors in Hong Kong SAR is one of the most expensive in the world. It is about 11 times per capita GDP and five times as expensive as those for secondary school teachers. In addition, remuneration packages are equalized across different academic fields.

---

[13]In FY2001, fewer than 50 percent of teachers in government and government-aided primary schools and 80 percent of teachers in secondary schools were university graduates.

Table 3.4. Estimated Comprehensive Social Security Assistance (CSSA) Expenditure, by Type of Case, FY1995–FY2002
(In millions of Hong Kong dollars)

Fiscal Year	Old Age	Disability/Ill Health	Single-Parent Family	Low Earnings	Unemployment	Others	Total
1995	2,705	952	609	97	237	232	4,831
1996	3,592	1,376	1,041	207	535	378	7,128
1997	4,570	1,784	1,482	340	784	482	9,441
1998	6,124	2,280	2,345	573	1,537	169	13,029
1999	7,030	1,957	2,317	624	1,495	200	13,623
2000	7,211	1,975	2,274	649	1,250	201	13,560
2001	7,538	2,104	2,476	671	1,420	195	14,405
2002	7,868	2,286	2,839	754	2,178	205	16,131

Source: Hong Kong SAR authorities.

The need for Hong Kong SAR to upgrade the skill level of its labor force will create new demands on educational spending in the near term. For example, if the current unit cost for higher education is maintained, doubling the university enrollment rate to 34 percent would imply additional educational spending of HK$13 billion (1.1 percent of GDP). Furthermore, to increase the percentage of college-degree holders among primary and secondary teachers, as has been set out as an objective by the government, would also have significant budgetary implications.

Health Care

Health care expenditures, the third-largest spending item in the government budget, have grown by more than 6 percent annually in real terms since FY1996, partly because of the aging of the population.[14] As a percentage of GDP and as a percentage of total government expenditure, health care spending in Hong Kong SAR is not high by OECD standards. However, based on current population trends, public health spending is projected to double by 2015 and may account for as much as 20–22 percent of total government expenditure.[15]

Fees in public hospitals and clinics are heavily subsidized and have not risen in line with costs. The fee structure is uniform, irrespective of the individual patient's ability to pay, but fees may be reduced or waived in cases of financial hardship. The government finances 97 percent of inpatient costs and 93 percent of outpatient costs in public health care facilities. In total, user fees paid by patients finance less than 5 percent of public health expenditures.

Welfare

Welfare spending has grown rapidly in the last decade, reflecting rising cash and housing assistance to the elderly, immigrants from mainland China, and the unemployed (Table 3.4). The number of recipients of Comprehensive Social Security Assistance (CSSA) has grown progressively since the program's introduction in 1993, and nominal payments have not been adjusted in line with deflation over the past four years. There are concerns that the benefit levels have become increasingly attractive vis-à-vis wages.

Options for Controlling Expenditures

Affordability within a tightening budget constraint has become a dominant consideration for governments in many industrial countries when allocating public resources among different policy areas. Although there are no available economic theories that can lay out optimal public resource allocations, experiences of other industrial countries can be helpful in identifying areas for possible expenditure cuts and rationalizations.

The FY2003 budget has set the target for expenditure reductions by FY2006 at HK$20 billion, which would amount to a 10 percent reduction in total expenditures. In the FY2003 budget, the government

[14]Traditionally, housing has been an important public spending item, but it is not included in social spending in this paper.

[15]See Harvard Consultancy Team, 1999, "Improving Hong Kong SAR's Health Care System: Why and for Whom?" (Hong Kong SAR: Health and Welfare Bureau).

has identified a number of areas for expenditure reductions. Further reductions may be required in these and other areas to achieve the targeted expenditure cuts.

- Recent developments in civil-service pay, particularly compared with pay in the private sector, and the changing economic situation in Hong Kong SAR highlight the need for reform. It is generally acknowledged that a good civil-service-pay system helps attract and retain talent and reduce corruption. The public sector wage bill, which accounts for a substantial share of operating expenditures, may, however, have to be reduced significantly to achieve the targeted fiscal consolidation. The FY2003 budget has proposed a 6 percent cut in the public sector wage bill and a 10 percent cut in the civil-service workforce. These measures are expected to yield HK$12 billion in savings. The government should also consider delinking the pay system for employees in government-funded organizations from that of the civil service to reduce wage rigidity in the public sector. Moreover, completing the pay-level survey expeditiously would help facilitate the process of further rationalizing civil servants' compensation.

- Given the weak fiscal position, a major change in the structure of educational finance is needed to improve the quality of basic education and expand higher education. Areas of improvement could include (1) adjusting the distribution of spending among different levels of education, with more resources allocated to basic education; (2) promoting private provision of education; (3) experimenting with a voucher system; (4) substantially increasing fees charged for tertiary education; and (5) recruiting more tuition-paying university students from mainland China (in effect, exporting education services). Furthermore, although the quality of education is difficult to assess, especially at the university level, the high per-student spending warrants further review of the pay system for university professors. Teacher salaries should be delinked from civil-service pay and aligned more closely with international norms.

- Greater burden sharing with the private sector is needed to keep the government's share of health expenditure steady at its current level of 2½ percent of GDP. This could be achieved through higher user fees, introducing means testing, and encouraging more private insurance. Also, given the higher quality of health care services in Hong Kong SAR, high-income individuals from the mainland could be attracted to come and use the health care services (in effect, exporting

health care services). The government has already taken a number of steps in these areas. It has also commissioned a comprehensive review of the existing fee structure in the public health care sector to achieve better targeting and prioritizing of finite public subsidies to the most needy.

- Some adjustments in the CSSA program appear warranted if the spiraling welfare budget is to be controlled. The FY2003 budget proposed an 11.1 percent reduction in welfare benefits. The government has also taken initiatives to encourage capable CSSA recipients to become self reliant. Some restructuring of this program, such as reducing the length and replacement ratio of benefits for able-bodied individuals, may, however, be needed to mitigate disincentive effects that could dissuade them from actively seeking reemployment and that may have contributed to rising long-term unemployment.

Conclusions

During the last decade, Hong Kong SAR has undergone a tremendous change in its public finances. On the one hand, the scale, expenditure, and outcome of its provision of social services have improved significantly. Housing, medical, educational, and social welfare services have gradually become a vital part of the social fabric. On the other hand, Hong Kong SAR's narrow tax base and heavy reliance on asset-related revenues have constrained the government's ability to finance its recurrent expenditures, especially during economic downturns.

Fiscal policy in Hong Kong SAR has reached a critical stage. The mounting deficits have already raised concerns in international and local markets. Concrete and credible measures to rein in the deficits are therefore crucial for the long-term sustainability of the public finances and the stability of the linked exchange rate system. The medium-term fiscal consolidation program in Hong Kong SAR has to strike a balance between the need to provide comprehensive social services to its citizens and its tradition of limiting the size and role of the government in economic and social affairs. On the one hand, if Hong Kong SAR wants to maintain a small government by keeping its current revenue system, major reforms are needed in the civil service and social services (education, health care, and welfare) to bring the government expenditure-to-GDP ratio back to the 16–17 percent range. On the other hand, if the current level and coverage of social services are to be maintained or expanded, taxes will have to be raised significantly.

Appendix. Assumptions for Medium-Term Projections

Table A.3.1. Assumptions for Medium-Term Projections

	Fiscal Year				
	2003	2004	2005	2006	2007
	(In percent)				
Basic Assumptions[1]					
Real GDP growth	2.2	3.1	3.4	3.8	3.5
CPI inflation	−2.0	−1.4	−0.7	−0.1	0.0
GDP deflator	−1.9	−1.0	−0.7	−0.2	−0.2

	FY2004–FY2007
Recurrent revenue items	Growth rate = growth rate of nominal GDP
Land premium[2]	2 percent of annual GDP
Investment income	5 percent nominal return on fiscal reserves
Other capital revenue[2]	0.8 percent of annual GDP
Social security expenditure[2]	Growth rate = $0.44 * CPI * $ portion of population age 65 and older

No-Policy-Action Scenario	FY2003–FY2007
Revenue	No revenue efforts
Government expenditure excluding social security expenditure[2]	Growth rate = growth rate of nominal GDP + 0.8 percent

Scenario 1	FY2003	FY2004	FY2005
Additional revenue from proposed measures in FY2003 budget *(billion Hong Kong dollars)*	6	13	14

	FY2004–FY2006	FY2007 onward
Government expenditure excluding social security expenditure *(in percent)*	−9.0	Growth rate = growth rate of nominal GDP

Scenario 2	FY2003	FY2004	FY2005
Additional revenue from proposed measures in FY2003 budget *(billion Hong Kong dollars)*	6	13	14
Goods and services tax *(billion Hong Kong dollars)*			18

	FY2004–FY2006	FY2007 onward
Government expenditure excluding social security expenditure *(in percent)*	−5.7	Growth rate = growth rate of nominal GDP

Note: CPI denotes the consumer price index.

[1]Demographic parameters are based on *Hong Kong SAR Population Projections 2000–2029* and Hong Kong SAR's 2001 *Population Census*.

[2]Parameters are drawn from the budget model in the *Final Report* by Hong Kong SAR's Task Force on Review of Public Finances (2002).

IV Determinants of, and Prospects for, Property Prices

Jorge Chan-Lau

The evolution of property prices has important implications for macroeconomic outcomes in Hong Kong SAR. Property price declines, such as those experienced during the past five years, have been amplified through balance-sheet effects, thereby depressing consumption and investment. On the fiscal front, government revenues from land leases have declined substantially as developers have lowered their reservation prices. Finally, the decline in property prices has also contributed to the continued deflation in the region. An assessment of the outlook for property prices in Hong Kong SAR is thus of considerable importance from a broader macroeconomic perspective.

Recovery in the property sector will depend upon both domestic and global economic conditions, as well as on successful integration with the mainland of China. On the one hand, although the inventory of unsold units and vacant office and commercial space remains relatively high by historical standards, a strong economic recovery and the associated boost in aggregate demand could go a long way toward correcting the imbalances. On the other hand, excess property inventory could continue to pose a major problem for the recovery of the aggregate price level in a weak economy.

In the near term, supply factors could contribute to reducing excess inventory in the residential market and relieve some of the downward price pressure. Starting in 2003, the supply of government-subsidized housing will be scaled down drastically. Also, private construction will likely slow down. Although the possible effects of continued price convergence with the mainland remain a concern, most market analysts believe that the availability of low-cost housing in Shenzhen does not contribute to increased effective supply in the housing market of Hong Kong SAR. In their view, the existence of a "Hong Kong SAR premium" is justified by the region's lower crime rate and better medical care and education services.

Econometric analysis suggests that current housing prices are approximately consistent with fundamental factors; future prospects remain uncertain, however. Results obtained using different model specifications and a variety of scenarios suggest that current prices are approximately in line with demand-side fundamentals. Continued weaknesses in housing prices cannot be ruled out, however, unless the economic recovery strengthens significantly.

Macroeconomic Implications of Changes in Property Prices

The macroeconomic impacts of changes in property prices in Hong Kong SAR have been quantified recently by Peng, Cheung, and Leung (2001), based on data for 1984–2000. Their results indicate that a 10 percent drop in property prices reduces private consumption growth by 1 percentage point and investment growth by one-fourth of 1 percentage point, after controlling for the effects of other variables including changes in GDP and asset prices. Empirical evidence also suggests that total bank lending adjusts to changes in property prices (Gerlach and Peng, 2002), supporting the view that there is a "balance-sheet" or "net-worth" channel through which property prices play an important role in determining the demand for credit.[1]

Government revenue in Hong Kong SAR is highly dependent on property-related income through both land sales and stamp duties. The dwindling demand for housing has, in turn, reduced developers' demand for land and contributed to lower land prices. Revenues from stamp duties have fallen as a result of lower property prices and reduced transaction volumes. The suspension of land sales announced in November 2002, although intended to redress the

---

[1]The "balance-sheet" or "net-worth" channel view explains the relationship between asset prices and economic activity through the value of collateral: in the presence of credit-market frictions, access to credit depends on the ability of the borrower to collateralize the loan, which, in turn, depends on current asset prices. This channel gives rise to a "financial accelerator" mechanism: declines in asset prices reduce creditworthiness, and the contraction in credit causes a fall in consumption and investment. Future economic activity is negatively affected, which, in turn, increases downward pressure on asset prices. See Kiyotaki and Moore (1997) and Bernanke and others (1999).

Figure 4.1. Property Price Indices
(1980: Q1 = 100)

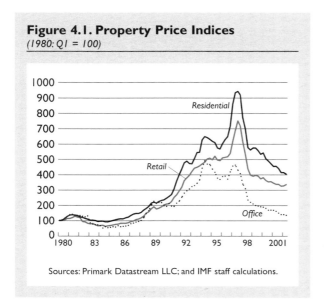

Sources: Primark Datastream LLC; and IMF staff calculations.

Figure 4.2. Rental Indices
(1980: Q1 = 100)

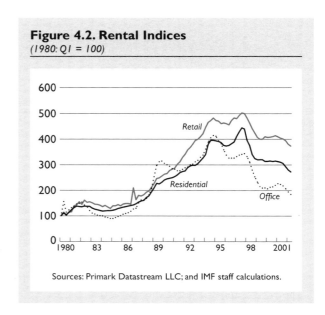

Sources: Primark Datastream LLC; and IMF staff calculations.

imbalance in property market prices, has cut off one important source of revenues just when the government faces serious fiscal challenges.

The stock market has been affected by the decline in property prices, since real estate firms account for more than 20 percent of total market capitalization. Hence, developments in the property sector affect both households' and banks' investment portfolios. In addition, market analysts have reported that the aggregate real estate exposures of the five largest Hong Kong SAR banks range between 20 and 40 percent of their equity bases. It is believed, however, that banks' earnings and equity bases could withstand further property price declines of 10–15 percent without a significant increase in their vulnerability.[2]

At the same time, the decline of property prices in Hong Kong SAR has helped to improve competitiveness. But office-occupancy costs are still high relative to other financial centers in the region. A recent survey indicates that by the end of 2002, occupancy costs of US$59 per square foot per annum made Hong Kong SAR the second most expensive city in East Asia. In contrast, annual office-occupancy costs in Beijing, Singapore, and Shenzhen were US$41, US$34, and US$29 per square foot, respectively.

Recent Developments in Property Market

Prices in the property market, regardless of sectoral and geographic distribution, have experienced a sustained decline since their peak in 1997 (Figure 4.1).[3] The main reasons for this decline are widely considered to be the weak economic performance of Hong Kong SAR's economy following the financial turbulence in 1997–98; overbuilding; and, possibly, increased integration with the mainland.

The year 2002 witnessed a significant pickup in the volume of primary market transactions in the residential sector, owing to the low-interest-rate environment. High affordability ratios and mortgage rates at subprime levels helped primary-market sales to reach a four-year high of 27,000 units in 2002, well above the annual average of 19,000 units for 1999–2001. Prices have continued to decline, however, because of aggressive sales tactics including price cuts, cash rebates, and developer-provided subsidies. Increased sales in the primary market have come at the expense of reduced transactions in the secondary market, where transactions declined by 5 percent in 2002.

Excess vacant office space and weak demand have caused rental rates for office space to fall steadily, dropping by more than 50 percent since their 1997 peaks (Figure 4.2). Weak global economic conditions have depressed the business prospects of the financial services, insurance, and trading industries and reduced demand for office space. As a result, vacancy rates reached 10 percent by the third quarter of 2002, well above the 4 percent average vacancy rate seen before the Asian crisis. In the next two years, the completion of new office buildings is expected to increase the inventory of available office space and contribute to keeping rental rates down.

---

[2]Morgan Stanley (2002).

[3]HSBC (2002).

In the past year, rental rates in the retail sector have been less affected than in the office sector owing to increased spending on tourism, especially by visitors from the mainland, which helped to offset faltering domestic consumption. Properties located close to major transportation hubs and enjoying high foot traffic benefited the most. Excess inventory is less of a problem in this sector.

Government Measures

In the past, the government has played an active role in the property market by supplying subsidized housing and controlling the land supply. Table 4.1 chronicles the major measures that have targeted the housing sector since 1997. Since 1998, the government has reduced its role as a provider of subsidized public housing while encouraging private house ownership. On November 13, 2002, the government unveiled a property policy package focused on the supply side of the market.

Two important measures included in the November 2002 policy package were the temporary halt in land sales, through the suspension of the scheduled land auctions and the Application List and tenders from the Mass Transit Railway Corporation (MTRC) and the Kowloon-Canton Railway Corporation (KCRC), until the end of 2003; and the termination of the construction and sale of flats under the Home Ownership Scheme (HOS) from 2003 onward. In the short term, these measures are likely to have only a negligible impact on housing prices, since most residential construction that will be completed during the next three years has already been started.

On January 2, 2003, the government implemented the new Home Assistance Loan Scheme (HALS). This scheme provides no-interest loans to low-income families for the purchase of private residential units and replaces two similar schemes, the Home Purchase Loan Scheme (HPLS) and the Home Starter Loan Scheme (HSLS). The HALS's main differences from the previous schemes are the lowering of the maximum income ceiling for families not living in public housing units and a general reduction in loan amounts to account for the decline in property prices. The initial quota is 10,000 cases per year, though it is difficult to project whether the quota will be fully used. Although the new scheme provides incentives for purchasing private units, past experience with the HPLS suggests that the HALS quota may not be fully used.

Starting in 2004, land sales will be triggered only through the application list system. Under this system, the government announces in advance what lots will be available for sale (by auction or tender) in the coming year. An interested party can trigger the auction of a lot by submitting a price bid acceptable to

Table 4.1. Major Policy Measures in Property Market, 1997–2003

October 1997	Housing Policy Plan aimed at increasing home ownership. Key measures include increasing land supply, increased supply of subsidized housing, non-interest loans through the Home Starter Loan Scheme (HSLS), and shortening of waiting time for public rental housing.
May 1998	Relaxation of anti-speculative administrative measures on the sale and presale of apartments.
June 1998	Suspension of land sales for nine months.
September 1998	Further relaxation of anti-speculative measures by removing restrictions on deposits and payments on the purchase of apartments.
April 1999	Resumption of land sale. Introduction of the application list system.
June 2000	Reduction in supply of subsidized apartments; increase in subsidized loans.
February 2001	Tightening of eligibility requirements for subsidized apartments; further relaxation of anti-speculative measures.
September 2001	Nine-month moratorium on Home Ownership Scheme (HOS)/Private Sector Participation Scheme (PSPS) sales replaced by additional home-ownership loans; administrative freeze on allocation of new sites for HOS/PSPS development.
June 2002	Resumption of HOS sales but supply reduced.
November 2002	Moratorium on land sales until after 2003; phaseout of HOS after the end of 2003; land sales conducted only through the application list starting 2004.
January 2003	Replacement of Home Purchase Loan Scheme (HPLS) and HSLS with Home Assistance Loan Scheme (HALS): tightening of maximum income eligibility for those not living in public rental housing; lowering of maximum loan amount.

Sources: Hong Kong SAR government publications; Morgan Stanley Dean Witter.

the government. The land is then auctioned or tendered publicly to the highest bidder. In the absence of other interested parties, the party that triggers the auction is awarded the land for the price it bid, after acceptance by the government.

Fundamental Housing Prices

Fundamental prices in the residential sector are estimated using the methodology first proposed by Abraham and Hendershott (1996) and subsequently used by Kalra and others (2000) and Peng (2002). Using this methodology, the growth rate of property prices can be decomposed into a fundamental component, which is a linear function of variables determining demand and supply, and a bubble component, which is a function of lagged prices and the gap between fundamental and past price levels.

Following the econometric specification of Kalra and others (2000), it is assumed that the growth rate in residential property prices, p, can be decomposed into the growth rate of the fundamental or equilibrium price, p^*, and an adjustment term, θ:

$$p_t = p_t^* + \theta_t. \tag{1}$$

The fundamental price growth rate is a linear function of changes in disposable real income or some appropriate proxy, dpi, contemporaneous and lagged values of changes in the real rental rate, rr, and the level of the real best lending rate, blr, which is a proxy for mortgage rates:

$$p_t^* = \alpha_0 + \alpha_1 dpi_t + \alpha_2 rr_t + \alpha_3 rr_{t-1} + \alpha_4 rr_{t-2} + \alpha_5 blr_t. \tag{2}$$

The adjustment term, θ, is given by the following equation:

$$\theta_t = \lambda_0 + \lambda_1 p_{t-1} + \lambda_2 (\log P_{t-1} - \log P_{t-1}^*) + \varepsilon_t, \tag{3}$$

where P and P^* are the market and fundamental price, respectively, and ε is an i.i.d. (independent and indentically distributed) error term. The log difference of the market price and the fundamental price is defined as the *fundamental price gap*. If λ_1 is positive, the second term in equation (3) can be interpreted as a bubble component, since higher prices in the previous period are carried over to the next period. If λ_2 is negative, the third term in equation (3) can be interpreted as a mean-reverting term or "bubble-burster" that causes prices to revert to their fundamental values.

The choice of explanatory variables in equation (2) is guided by their role in determining housing demand. Equations (2) and (3) were estimated for three different specifications that differed in the choice of proxy for disposable income: real household disposable income, real GDP, and the unemployment rate. The estimation results for the three specifications are presented in Table 4.2, the corresponding paths for fundamental prices in Figure 4.3. It should be noted, though, that these results have been obtained from model specifications that include neither supply factors, such as the provision of public housing in the future, nor current excess inventory

of unsold units.[4] In addition, the availability of cheaper housing across the border in Shenzhen has not been included explicitly in the model because of a lack of historical data.

Table 4.2 shows that for the three different model specifications analyzed, all explanatory variables enter with the expected sign and are statistically significant. Furthermore, the magnitudes of the coefficients on all explanatory variables, excluding the proxy for disposable income, are rather similar across different model specifications. The results

Table 4.2. Speculative-Bubble Model of Real Property Prices

Variable	(1)	(2)	(3)
Constant	0.017* (0.009)	0.006 (0.008)	0.024* (0.007)
Real disposable income	0.264** (0.160)	...	...
Real GDP growth rate	...	0.434* (0.138)	...
Changes in unemployment rate	...	...	−0.023** (0.013)
Change in real rental rate	1.115* (0.222)	0.848* (0.230)	1.028* (0.216)
Change in real rental rate (−1)	−0.820* (0.260)	−0.847* (0.245)	−0.691* (0.239)
Change in real rental rate (−2)	0.023 (0.214)	−0.002 (0.207)	0.071 (0.207)
Best lending rate	−0.454* (0.132)	−0.408* (0.121)	−0.480* (0.127)
Change in real housing price (−1)	0.381* (0.129)	0.378* (0.134)	0.382* (0.130)
Fundamental price gap	−0.182* (0.064)	−0.213* (0.068)	−0.204* (0.067)
Adjusted R-squared	0.61	0.61	0.62
Standard error of regression	0.04	0.04	0.04
Durbin-Watson statistic	2.16	2.05	2.14
Number of observations	66.00	66.00	66.00

Sources: Primark Datastream LLC; and IMF staff calculations.
Notes: The only difference among the three specifications shown in this table is the choice of proxy for disposable income. * denotes significance at 5 percent confidence level. ** denotes significance at 10 percent confidence level.

---

[4]This shortcoming is addressed in the study by Peng (2002). The results reported here, however, are similar to those reported in the Peng study. Furthermore, the use of the best lending rate rather than the mortgage-rate series used by Peng did not alter the results substantially.

Figure 4.3. Residential Property Prices
(Logarithm of price index, 1980: Q1 = 100)

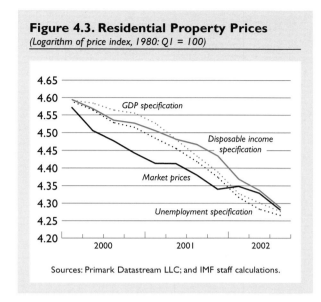

Sources: Primark Datastream LLC; and IMF staff calculations.

suggest that bubbles in the housing market in Hong Kong SAR occurred in the past, since, ceteris paribus, a 1 percent change in housing prices results in a 2½ percent increase in property prices in the long run. The bubble-burster coefficient associated with the fundamental price gap is negative, however, which suggests the existence of price-correction mechanisms in the housing market. These results are

consistent with previous findings by Kalra and others (2000) and Peng (2002).

Figure 4.3 shows that from the first quarter of 2000 until the first quarter of 2002, housing prices in Hong Kong SAR were below levels consistent with fundamental demand factors (fundamental levels) for all model specifications. During 2002, different model specifications delivered different conclusions. On the one hand, housing prices are just one-half of 1 percent above fundamental levels according to the disposable-income specification. On the other hand, the GDP and unemployment specifications suggest that housing prices are undervalued by one-half of 1 percent and 1½ percent, respectively, relative to fundamental levels. But note that the differences in results across these alternative specifications are quite small.[5] Overall, given data-measurement errors and uncertainty regarding the correct specification of the model, it seems reasonable to assert that by the third quarter of 2002, housing prices were approximately in line with fundamentals.

Uncertainty in the model-parameter estimates as well as in the macroeconomic forecasts suggests that out-of-sample projections from these model specifications should be interpreted with considerable caution. Table 4.3 provides some illustrative calcula-

---

[5]The standard deviation of the point estimates ranges between 0.60 and 0.70.

Table 4.3. Scenarios for Housing-Price Projections
(In percentage points)

	Scenario 1 (Benchmark)		Scenario 2		Scenario 3		Scenario 4	
	2003	2004	2003	2004	2003	2004	2003	2004
GDP specification								
Assumptions								
Real GDP growth	2.2	3.1	4.5	6.0	2.2	3.1	2.2	3.1
Best lending rate	7.0	7.0	7.0	7.0	7.0	5.0	7.0	7.0
Real rental rate growth	−2.0	−2.0	−2.0	−2.0	−2.0	−2.0	0.0	5.0
Implied price changes								
Market prices	−7.2	−3.5	−2.2	2.9	−5.9	0.0	−3.3	0.0
Fundamental prices	−5.3	−3.8	−1.3	1.3	−4.3	−1.1	−2.3	−0.7
Unemployment specification								
Assumptions								
Unemployment rate	7.4	7.0	7.0	6.8	7.4	7.0	7.4	7.0
Best lending rate	7.0	7.0	7.0	7.0	7.0	5.0	7.0	7.0
Real rental rate growth	−2.0	−2.0	−2.0	−2.0	−2.0	−2.0	0.0	5.0
Implied price changes								
Market prices	−11.6	−6.7	−10.4	−7.4	−10.1	−2.7	−4.5	7.5
Fundamental prices	−7.9	−6.5	−7.0	−7.0	−6.7	−3.4	−2.3	4.8

Sources: Primark Datastream LLC; and IMF staff calculations.

tions to show how, using IMF staff projections of real GDP growth and unemployment rates, the GDP and unemployment specifications can be used to project how fundamental prices and market prices would evolve under different scenarios. These scenarios suggest that additional small declines in fundamental prices may occur in 2003 if the economy remains weak. Fundamental prices are projected to increase, however, especially in 2004, if GDP growth and/or rental rates strengthen significantly. It is worth reemphasizing, in this context, that the evolution of supply factors could substantially alter the price dynamics predicted by this model, which does not account explicitly for the impact of such factors. Further work integrating both demand factors and supply factors could be helpful, particularly in analyzing the impact of property prices in neighboring Shenzhen on property prices in Hong Kong SAR.

Conclusions

The analysis undertaken in this section suggests that in the housing market, prices are roughly at levels consistent with those determined by demand factors such as personal disposable income, rental rates, and interest rates. This analysis has focused on demand-side factors, since updated and historically consistent data on key supply-side variables were difficult to obtain. Nevertheless, the results are in line with those reported in an earlier study by Peng (2002), which were obtained using a similar model that included supply-related explanatory variables. Although property prices now appear to be at levels consistent with demand-side fundamentals, further weaknesses in housing prices cannot be ruled out if Hong Kong SAR's economy remains weak.

V Deflation Dynamics

Papa N'Diaye

Hong Kong SAR has experienced continued deflation since the last quarter of 1998. The composite consumer price index (CPI) fell by almost 14 percent from the third quarter of 1998 until December 2002; about half of this deflation is accounted for by the decline in housing costs, following the bursting of the bubble in property prices that had built up in the mid-1990s.[1] Other items that have also contributed significantly to the decline in prices include food, clothing and footwear, and durable goods (Table 5.1). Falling prices have contributed to increased real debt burdens, depressed consumer confidence, and tightened monetary conditions, and could have helped feed the contraction in aggregate demand (Table 5.2).

Previous research has suggested that although structural factors have played a role, deflation was mainly attributable to cyclical factors. Analysis carried out by the IMF staff during the 2002 Article IV consultation with Hong Kong SAR showed that fluctuations in unemployment, nominal credit, and the nominal effective exchange rate—which were considered cyclical variables—were the main determinants of the decline in prices (IMF (2002), Chapter III). This result implies that as these cyclical factors turn around, deflation will end. Research by the Hong Kong Monetary Authority (HKMA, 2001) arrived at similar conclusions.

The persistence of deflation for such an extended period of time suggests, however, that other factors may be in play. In general, an economy's cyclical condition, as measured for instance by the output gap, can be affected by both transitory and permanent shocks, the relative importance of which determines the persistence of deflation. For example, as deflation increases the real debt burden and becomes entrenched in expectations, private investment and consumption growth could decline, causing an even greater decline in economic activity.

This section presents a more comprehensive analysis, which provides a decomposition of the aggregate price level into transitory and permanent components, and identifies the nature and origin of the shocks that drive these two components. The analysis is based on a methodology with several features that are useful for analyzing deflation and its persistence. First, it provides a clear distinction between those driving forces behind deflation that create trend movements in the variables (summarized in the permanent component) and those that generate temporary deviations from long-run equilibrium conditions (summarized in the transitory component). Second, it provides a framework for identifying the nature of those forces. The approach undertaken here is a "structural" one, as opposed to the commonly used reduced-form approach. It helps, for example, to determine whether falling prices result from one or more of the following: increased productivity, scarce money supply, and temporary excess capacity. This is particularly relevant, because the likely duration of deflation, its costs, and the policy actions that may be needed to combat it all depend upon the nature of the deflation's underlying causes.

Empirical evidence suggests that the contribution of the permanent component has become relatively more important over time in explaining deflation. The sustained fall in the aggregate price level is mostly accounted for by continuous declines in its permanent component, which summarizes the cumulative effects of productivity shocks, scarce money supply, and price convergence with trading partners. These findings indicate that although the transitory component did contribute significantly to the initial phase of deflation, its effects are becoming progressively weaker.

Framework

A structural vector error-correction-modeling approach à la King and others (1991) is used to assess the nature and impact of shocks on prices to shed light on the main factors that are behind their sus-

---

[1]July 2003 figures indicate that deflation is continuing: prices fell by 4.0 percent year on year, although this sharp decline is partly attributable to temporary utility rate concessions granted by the government.

Table 5.1. Contributors to Deflation

	Weight	Cumulative Change Sep. 1998–Dec. 2002 (percent)[1]	Contribution to Overall Deflation (percentage points)	Contribution to Overall Deflation (share)
Composite CPI[2]	100.0	–13.7	–13.7	100.0
Of which:				
Food	26.7	–7.7	–2.1	15.0
Housing	29.9	–26.2	–7.8	57.3
Electricity, gas, and water	3.0	–5.0	–0.2	1.1
Alcoholic drinks and tobacco	0.9	5.1	0.0	–0.4
Clothing and footwear	4.1	–35.5	–1.5	10.7
Durable goods	6.2	–27.2	–1.7	12.4
Miscellaneous goods	5.7	3.7	0.2	–1.6
Transport	9.0	–0.2	0.0	0.1
Miscellaneous services	14.4	–4.9	–0.7	5.2

Sources: Data from CEIC Data Co., Ltd. database; and IMF staff calculations.

[1]Based on log-difference approximation.

[2]CPI denotes the consumer price index. Sum of the components using fixed weights over the period September 1998 through December 2002.

tained decline. The structural vector error-correction model, also known as the common-trends model (CTM), is well suited for analyzing the interaction between variables that display trends and are determined simultaneously, uses general restrictions derived from economic theory to identify the main driving forces behind the trends observed in aggregate macroeconomic variables, and ensures consis-

tency between the short-run and long-run dynamics of those variables.

The CTM includes the following variables: real output, measured as nominal GDP deflated by the (composite) consumer price index; broad money; the consumer price index; real asset prices, measured by the Hang Seng stock index deflated by the consumer price index; and foreign prices in Hong Kong dollars (HK$), measured as the trading partners' consumer price indices expressed in HK$.[2]

Figure 5.1 provides a diagrammatic representation of this framework. It shows how the outturn of the price level can be decomposed into two components that reflect its short-run and trend movements, and that can be used to identify their main driving forces.

- Panel I displays several possible factors that could, at each point in time, influence different sides of the economy (for example, supply versus demand and nominal versus real).

- The occurrence of an event related to these factors constitutes a "shock." The nature of the shocks is determined according to which side of

Table 5.2. Some Key Economic Indicators
(Year-on-year percentage change, unless otherwise indicated)

	Period Average, 1993: Q3–1997: Q3	Period Average, 1998: Q3–2002: Q4
Real GDP	5.03	3.00
Real domestic demand	7.03	–0.33
Real consumption	4.96	0.49
Real gross fixed capital formation	11.17	–3.08
Real interest rates[1]	0.38	10.60
Real interest rates[2]	–2.71	6.95
Unemployment rate[3]	2.20	7.20

Sources: CEIC Data Co., Ltd. database; Hong Kong SAR authorities; and IMF staff calculations.

[1]Best lending rate *minus* actual year-on-year consumer price index (CPI) inflation.

[2]Interbank offered rate *minus* actual year-on-year CPI inflation.

[3]Levels of unemployment rate prevailing in 1997: Q3 and 2002: Q4.

[2]There are three main reasons why stock prices have been used in lieu of property prices. First, the former ensure consistency with the predictions of economic theories that suggest the existence of a stable long-run arbitrage relationship between output and real stock prices (see, for example, Blanchard, 1981). Second, it provides a means for capturing, in a broad sense, the effects of changes in asset prices on both the corporate sector's balance sheets and households' wealth. Third, stock prices are highly correlated with property prices—the correlation between stock prices and property prices over 1980: Q4–2002: Q3 is 0.85, suggesting that this approach might not be too restrictive in any case.

Figure 5.1. Effects of Shocks on Prices

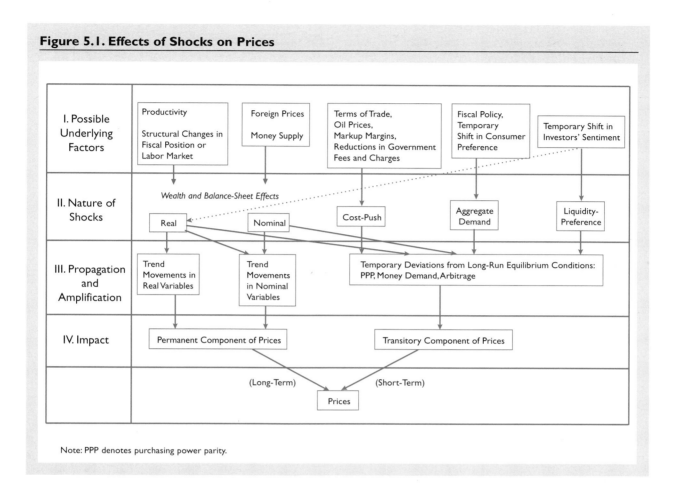

Note: PPP denotes purchasing power parity.

the economy they first have an impact on, as well as the temporal nature of the shock (see Panel II). There are two types of shock: transitory shocks, which generate only short-run movements in the variables, and permanent shocks, which generate both short-run and trend movements in the variables.[3] The transitory shocks are cost-push shocks (for example, changes in markup margins), aggregate-demand shocks (for example, temporary shifts in consumers' preferences), and liquidity-preference shocks. The permanent shocks are real (for example, productivity) shocks and changes in the money supply.[4]

- Each of these shocks generates particular movements in the variables of the system that distinguish it from the others (see Panel III). For example, the "real" shock, which is related to factors such as productivity changes or labor market reforms, generates short-run movements (for example, deviations from long-run equilibrium conditions) and trend movements in all variables, whether the latter are real or nominal. The "nominal" shock generates short-run movements in all the variables and trends in only those variables that are nominal. The cost-push shock generates short-run movements in all variables but does not affect their trends.

- The distinction between these two types of shock constitutes the pillar of the decomposition of each variable into a transitory component and a permanent component (see Panel IV). For each variable, the combination of the short-run movements generated by both types of shock constitutes its transitory component, while that of the effects of the permanent shocks on its trend or long-run dynamics constitutes its permanent component.

---

[3]Note that even the transitory shocks could, through their effects on private sector balance sheets, have persistent effects on prices that last beyond the duration of the shocks themselves.

[4]The term "changes in the money supply" refers to increases (decreases) in the money supply beyond (below) what is required to finance long-run real GDP. It is also worth noting that real shocks could also include those changes in the supply of goods and services that are due to wealth/balance-sheet effects resulting from, for example, shifts in investors' sentiment.

Figure 5.2. Prices: Actual, Permanent, and Transitory Components

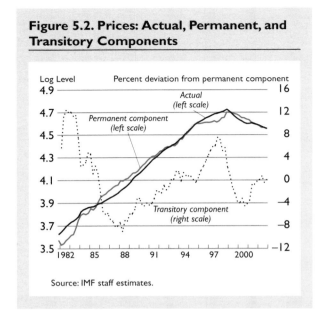

Source: IMF staff estimates.

Figure 5.3. Transitory Component of Prices: Contributions of Transitory Shocks
(In percent)

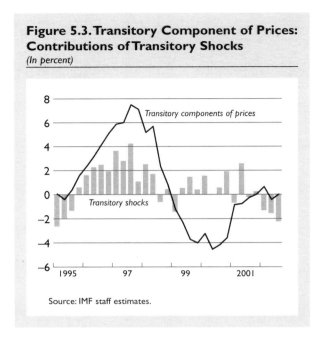

Source: IMF staff estimates.

The identification of the shocks that drive these two components is based on restrictions that are derived from economic theory. They include restrictions that stem from the long-run equilibrium relationships of a stable money demand, purchasing power parity (PPP), and arbitrage between output and real stock prices.[5] The money demand equation embeds the monetarist view that, in the long run, inflation/deflation is a monetary phenomenon. Purchasing power parity captures the effects of price convergence with trading partners. The arbitrage relationship between output and real stock prices captures the idea that certain developments in the real (supply) side of the economy, such as improved productivity or labor market reforms, can engender trends in asset prices because of their impact on current and prospective levels of corporate profitability. Additional restrictions that include the concept of long-run neutrality of money (vertical Phillips curve) and assumptions on stickiness in the adjustment process of certain variables to shocks are also used to obtain an exact identification of all shocks in the system.

The interpretation of the permanent and transitory components of each variable depends upon the effects of which shocks they include. For example, because the transitory component of output includes the short-run effects of productivity shocks, it can-

not be literally considered as a standard measure of output gap that would convey the notion of pressures arising from only the demand side of the economy.

Results

Over the 1998: Q4–2002: Q3 period, the decline in the price level has been associated with a decline in both its transitory and permanent components.[6] Although downward pressures on the price level resulting from the decline in the transitory component have been very pronounced during the initial phase of deflation, these have become progressively weaker. Consequently, most of the fall in the price level between 2001: Q3 and 2002: Q3 is accounted for by the decline in its permanent component (Figure 5.2).

The sustained fall in prices results mostly from the effects of permanent shocks that determine the path of the permanent component of prices and have a substantial impact on the transitory component. Over the deflation period, the effects of transitory shocks on the transitory component of prices have been outweighed by those of permanent shocks (Figure 5.3).[7] Shocks such as productivity shocks, changes in the money supply, and price equalization with trading

---

[5]These restrictions were tested jointly, since the Johansen maximum-likelihood estimation procedure indicated the existence of three cointegrating relationships. The PPP restriction, when tested separately, was not rejected at the 5 percent significance level. See Becker (1999) and Cassola and Morana (2002) for examples of studies using similar restrictions.

[6]The shocks that drive these two components are orthogonal by construction, but there is no restriction that the temporary and permanent components themselves be uncorrelated.

[7]The transitory component represents the temporary dynamic effects of all random disturbances and exogenous variables on the variables of the system.

Figure 5.4. Year-on-Year Inflation Rate: Actual, Permanent, and Transitory Components

(In percent)

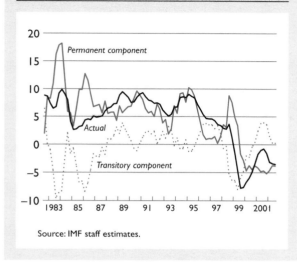

Source: IMF staff estimates.

partners have had a significant negative impact on the transitory component of prices over the period 1998: Q4–2002: Q3.

In terms of the rate of change in prices (that is, inflation or deflation), the estimates of the permanent component of prices show continued deflation owing to permanent shocks such as productivity shocks, changes in the money supply, and price equalization with trading partners over the last two years (see the graph of the permanent component in Figure 5.4).[8]

---

[8]The permanent component of the rate of change in prices has been obtained from the estimates of the permanent component of the price level displayed in Figure 5.2.

One approach to understanding the relative importance of different shocks is to examine their relative contributions to the variability of prices and output (Table 5.3).

Prices

Permanent shocks contribute 44 percent of the fluctuations in prices over the short term (one quarter) and 94 percent over the long term (40 quarters). The relative contributions of each of these shocks are as follows:

- Productivity shocks and shocks related to changes in the aggregate money supply and price equalization with trading partners account for 34 percent and 60 percent of the long-term fluctuations in prices, respectively.
- In the short (one quarter) and medium term (12 quarters), however, productivity shocks are the main sources of variability in prices, accounting for 39 percent and 44 percent of fluctuations in prices, respectively.

The contributions of transitory shocks represent about 56 percent of fluctuations in prices in the short term, which declines to about 35 percent in the medium term. They can be decomposed as follows:

- Cost-push shocks, which could reflect temporary changes in firms' markup margins or rates concessions and waivers of water and sewage charges granted by the government, contribute the most to the variability of prices. They explain about 55 percent of fluctuations in prices in the short term and about 13 percent in the medium term.
- Aggregate-demand shocks, such as discretionary fiscal policies or temporary changes in consumers' confidence, do not have an immediate effect on prices, but explain about 16 percent of their fluctuations in the medium term.
- The effects of liquidity-preference shocks on the aggregate level of prices are limited. Liquidity-

Table 5.3. Forecast Error Variance Decomposition

| | Permanent Shocks | | | | | | Transitory Shocks | | | | | | | | |
| | Real | | | Nominal | | | Liquidity-Preference | | | Cost-Push | | | Aggregate-Demand | | |
	S	M	L	S	M	L	S	M	L	S	M	L	S	M	L
Price level	0.39	0.44	0.34	0.05	0.21	0.60	0.00	0.06	0.01	0.55	0.13	0.03	0.01	0.16	0.03
Output	0.44	0.66	0.88	0.09	0.12	0.05	0.00	0.03	0.01	0.00	0.08	0.02	0.48	0.11	0.04
Money	0.13	0.27	0.52	0.63	0.58	0.41	0.23	0.12	0.05	0.00	0.01	0.01	0.01	0.02	0.01
Foreign price level	0.43	0.19	0.20	0.13	0.63	0.68	0.11	0.06	0.04	0.17	0.08	0.05	0.17	0.04	0.04
Real stock prices	0.49	0.57	0.67	0.09	0.06	0.08	0.42	0.27	0.17	0.00	0.07	0.05	0.00	0.03	0.03

Notes: S = short term (1 quarter); M = medium term (12 quarters); and L = long term (40 quarters).

preference shocks explain only about 6 percent of the fluctuations in prices in the medium term.[9]

Results (not reported here) of the historical decomposition of the price level into the components attributable to different shocks tell a similar story. Movements in the price level are largely determined by productivity shocks and shocks to the money supply and price equalization with trading partners.

Output

Permanent shocks contribute to 53 percent of output fluctuations in the short term and about 93 percent in the long term, the details of which are as follows:

- Real shocks (productivity shocks) and nominal shocks (changes in the aggregate money supply and price equalization with trading partners) explain 88 percent and 5 percent of output fluctuations in the long term, respectively. These shocks also account for an important part of its fluctuations in the short term: 44 percent and 9 percent, respectively.

The contributions of the transitory shocks represent 48 percent of output fluctuations in the short term and decline to about 22 percent over the medium term. The respective contributions of each transitory shock are as follows:

- Cost-push shocks account for 8 percent of the variability of output over the medium term.
- Aggregate-demand shocks explain about 48 percent of the short-term variability of output. Their relative contribution declines, however, to about 11 percent over the medium term.
- Liquidity-preference shocks explain only about 3 percent of the variability of output over the medium term.

Another approach to understanding the relative importance of shocks is to analyze their dynamic effects on prices. Such an analysis has several uses. First, it provides a means to verify the consistency of the effects of shocks with standard predictions of economic theory and, therefore, make an assessment of the validity of the identification restrictions used. Second, it provides information about how shocks are propagated and amplified throughout the economy. The dynamic effects on prices of one-time shocks of different types (Figure 5.5) suggest the following:

- The responses of prices to shocks are consistent with the predictions of standard economic theory. From an aggregate-supply/aggregate-demand perspective, a temporary real shock (for example, a one-time increase in supply owing to higher productivity) that, say, corresponds to an outward shift of the long-run aggregate-supply curve leads to a permanent decrease in prices (and an increase in output). A temporary negative aggregate-demand shock (of a Keynesian style) leads to an inward shift of the aggregate-demand curve that induces a fall in prices in the short run. With downward stickiness in wages, real wages increase, leading to a decline in output and higher unemployment. In the long run, as the aggregate-supply curve flattens, prices go back to their initial levels.[10]
- The adjustment of prices to transitory shocks is gradual, which suggests some degree of stickiness. The maximum effect is reached after seven quarters in response to an aggregate-demand shock, four quarters after a cost-push shock, and eight quarters after a liquidity-preference shock.[11]

Interpreting Results

The large relative contribution of permanent shocks (productivity, money supply/price convergence shocks) to fluctuations in prices, compared with that of temporary shocks such as aggregate-demand and cost-push shocks, probably reflects the increased degree of integration between Hong Kong SAR and the mainland of China and changes in the money supply.[12] This implies that downward pres-

---

[9]Because these transitory real-asset-price shocks do not create changes in households' wealth and/or corporate balance sheets that lead to permanent changes in output, they could reflect swings in investors' sentiment that affect the stock market without affecting the bond market significantly. Such shocks would leave market interest rates unchanged.

[10]Although the magnitudes and duration of the transitory effects of these shocks are determined empirically, their zero long-run impact on the price level is imposed by the identification scheme.

[11]Although the half-life of deviations from purchasing power parity appears not to be independent of the nature of the shocks that created it, estimates suggest a relatively fast speed of adjustment of the real exchange rate. It takes about eight quarters for half the effects of a cost-push shock to disappear, while half the effects of an aggregate-demand shock disappear only after 12 quarters.

[12]Under the linked exchange rate regime, changes in the U.S. federal funds rate lead to comparable changes in Hong Kong SAR's interest rate (Hong Kong interbank offered rate, or HIBOR). These changes imply adjustments in the monetary base to avoid capital flows that could put pressure on the exchange rate. The relative tightness of the monetary stance in the United States for Hong Kong SAR's economy can be inferred from the fact that the stock of broad money stood at or below its permanent level—that is, the level of broad money that is required to finance long-run real output—over the period 1996: Q1–2002: Q3.

Figure 5.5. Movements in Price Level in Response to Different One-Time Shocks

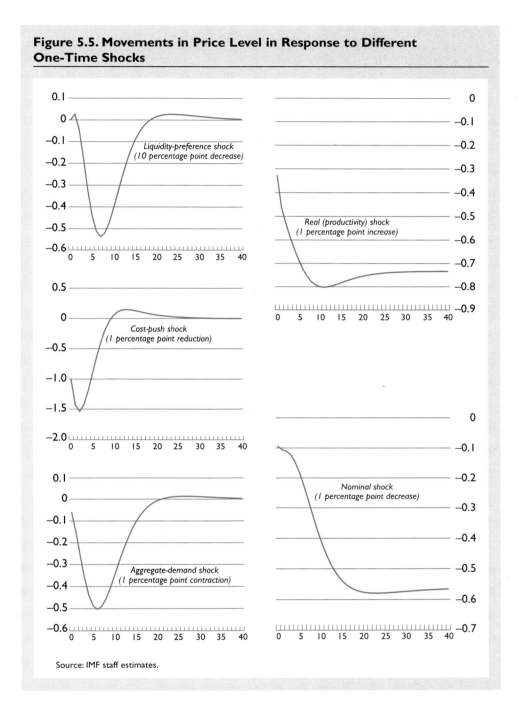

Source: IMF staff estimates.

sures could continue in the foreseeable future, since (1) price differentials between Hong Kong SAR and mainland cities such as Shenzhen and Guangdong remain substantial; and (2) the stance of monetary policy in the United States could tighten when the economy recovers. Moreover, given that wage differentials between Hong Kong SAR and the mainland cities have not narrowed substantially, the

convergence process is very likely to continue in the near future.

The limited contribution and duration of the impact of aggregate-demand shocks on prices, such as temporary fiscal measures, are consistent with evidence on the narrow tax structure and limited size of the fiscal multiplier in Hong Kong SAR. This result implies, however, that macroeconomic policy actions aimed at managing the demand side of the economy—in this case, expansionary fiscal policies—may be unlikely to have a significant direct effect on price developments.

Conclusions

The analysis in this section has shown that the effects of permanent shocks, such as productivity shocks and shocks related to changes in the money supply and price convergence with trading partners, have become more important over time in explaining deflation in Hong Kong SAR. These shocks originate partly from the real side of the economy (for example, changes in productivity) and partly from the monetary side, including the dynamic adjustment of prices for purchasing-power-parity purposes. In addition, the effects of temporary shifts in aggregate demand have been perpetuated by negative wealth and balance-sheet effects in the corporate and household sectors arising from asset-price declines over the past five years. The analysis has also shown that there is a prevalence of productivity and nominal shocks, such as changes in the money supply and price convergence with trading partners, in explaining price and output fluctuations.

VI Trends in Wage Inequality, 1981–2001

Dora Iakova

Income inequality in Hong Kong SAR has increased rapidly over the last twenty years (Figure 6.1). The Gini coefficient, a commonly used summary measure of household income inequality, rose from 0.451 in 1981 to 0.525 in 2001. At present, Hong Kong SAR ranks among the economies with the most uneven distributions of income in the world, even though income disparity has also widened in many other high-income economies over the last thirty years.[1] Rising wage inequality has been one of the driving forces behind the increase in household-income inequality.[2]

The main goal of this section is to document the evolution of wage inequality during 1981–2001.[3] The analysis indicates that the adjustment of the labor market to structural shifts was accompanied by an increase in wage disparity and a rise in returns to education. In this respect, developments in wage inequality are similar to those observed in the United States during the 1980s and 1990s. At the same time, real wages in Hong Kong SAR increased significantly across the entire distribution, reflecting positive spillovers from rapid economic growth. This finding contrasts with results for the United States, where rising wage inequality since the late 1970s has been characterized by *declining* real wages in the lower deciles of the wage distribution.

The last two decades were characterized by rapid structural change in Hong Kong SAR. Since the mainland opened to foreign investment in 1979, manufacturing production was gradually outsourced from

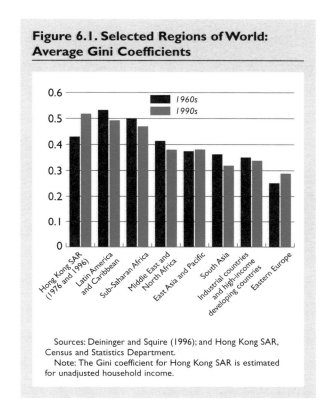

Figure 6.1. Selected Regions of World: Average Gini Coefficients

Sources: Deininger and Squire (1996); and Hong Kong SAR, Census and Statistics Department.
Note: The Gini coefficient for Hong Kong SAR is estimated for unadjusted household income.

Hong Kong SAR to the mainland, and there was a significant shift of employment toward the service sectors. Hong Kong SAR increasingly turned into an entrepôt center for mainland-produced manufacturing exports. The share of manufacturing value added declined to 5 percent of GDP from 23 percent between 1980 and 2000. Domestic goods exports declined to 14 percent of GDP from 48 percent, while reexports increased to 99 percent of GDP from 19 percent over the same period. The stages of production outsourced to the mainland were mostly those intensive in unskilled labor, while skill-intensive services related to manufacturing remained in Hong Kong SAR (see Feenstra and Hanson, 2001).

Examining the development of wage inequality over this period of massive relocation of production

---

[1]The World Bank's *World Development Report 1995* ranks Hong Kong SAR as having the highest rate of income inequality among high-income economies.

[2]Wages from main employment accounted for 89 percent of total household income in both 1981 and 2001 (based on a representative 1 percent sample from the Population Census).

[3]There are few studies of wage inequality in Hong Kong SAR. Suen (1995) examines the effect of a change in the industrial composition on the variance of wages over the period 1976–91. Liu (1997) provides a broad overview of household and wage inequality over the same period. In a recent paper, Hsieh and Woo (2000) attempt to quantify the impact of outsourcing on the shift in relative demand (and, therefore, on relative wages) for skilled workers in manufacturing over the period 1976–96.

Table 6.1. Summary Statistics for Wage-Analysis Sample, 1981–2001

	1981	1986	1991	1996	2001	Change 1981–2001
Number of observations	19,860	23,115	23,417	28,646	30,712	
Share of men	0.7	0.6	0.6	0.6	0.6	
Share of women	0.3	0.4	0.4	0.4	0.4	
Median (*log real wages*)	8.5	8.7	9.0	9.2	9.3	0.8
Men	8.6	8.8	9.1	9.2	9.4	0.8
Women	8.3	8.4	8.8	9.0	9.1	0.8
Mean (*log real wages*)	8.6	8.8	9.1	9.2	9.4	0.8
Men	8.7	8.9	9.2	9.3	9.5	0.8
Women	8.3	8.6	8.9	9.1	9.2	0.9

Sources: Hong Kong SAR Census; and IMF staff estimates.

is important, since it could shed light on the debate of the effect of globalization of production on relative wages. Feenstra and Hanson (1996) suggest that outsourcing of the low-skill-intensive stages of production within each industry would result in an increase in the relative demand for skilled labor. For Hong Kong SAR, the outsourcing of production to the mainland over the last two decades has been very significant. One rough measure of outsourcing is the size of outward-processing trade (involving raw materials export to the mainland for processing and a subsequent reimportation of processed goods). Such trade was nonexistent in the late 1970s, but by 2000 it accounted for 73 percent of Hong Kong SAR's domestic exports to the mainland, 79 percent of its imports from the mainland, and 85 percent of reexports originating on the mainland. Thus, it is likely that a substantial part of within-industry skill upgrading and of the increase in wage inequality in Hong Kong SAR is related to the process of outsourcing, and this section presents evidence in support of this theory.[4]

Evolution of Wage Inequality

Dataset

The dataset used in this section is constructed from a representative 1 percent sample of individuals

from the Hong Kong Population and By-Population Censuses conducted in 1981, 1986, 1991, 1996, and 2001. The data include information on after-tax monthly earnings from main and secondary employment, nonlabor income, industry sector of employment, occupation, education, demographics, and household characteristics for every individual. The wage variable examined is real monthly earnings from main employment. (The composite consumer price index, 1996 = 100, is used as the price deflator.) The analysis is restricted to employed people between 18 and 65 years of age.[5]

Summary statistics of the data are presented in Table 6.1. Median real monthly earnings increased significantly over the period 1981–2001, although the pace of growth of real earnings slowed between 1996 and 2001 in line with lower GDP growth. The share of women in the employed population increased by 10 percentage points over the period, reaching 45 percent in 2001.

There has been a significant shift of employment toward the service industries (Table 6.2). The share of manufacturing employment declined from 40 percent in 1981 to 12 percent in 2001, while the share of employment in the service sectors increased from 49 percent to 80 percent. Although an increasing employment share of services has been observed in most industrial countries in recent years, this shift

---

[4]Other explanations for rising wage disparity offered by the theoretical literature include skill-biased technological change, reductions in labor-market rigidities (such as minimum wages, strong unions, restrictive labor laws, and heavily progressive taxation of income), and growing trade with developing countries. See Wolff (2000) for a review of the literature.

[5]Hours worked are not reported in the data, so part-time workers are also included. The earnings data are top-coded. To eliminate outliers and top-coded observations, the bottom 1.5 percent and the top one-half of 1 percent of the wage distribution have been dropped for the purpose of this analysis. Sensitivity analysis has been performed by keeping all data points and adjusting the top-coded observations by assuming a Pareto distribution of the tail. Only the first three summary measures of wage inequality in Table 6.5 were affected by that adjustment.

Table 6.2. All Workers: Employment and Earnings, by Industry

	1981	1986	1991	1996	2001	Change, 1981–2001
			Share in Total Employment *(percent)*			
Utilities, agriculture	2.2	1.9	1.4	1.0	0.8	−1.4
Manufacturing	40.3	35.8	28.0	18.8	12.2	−28.1
Construction	8.9	6.3	6.9	7.9	7.5	−1.5
Wholesale, retail, hotels/restaurants	15.6	18.3	17.2	18.7	18.4	2.8
Import/export	3.3	4.1	4.4	6.2	7.5	4.3
Transport, storage, and communication	8.4	8.0	10.2	10.9	11.5	3.0
Financing, insurance, real estate, business services	5.4	6.5	11.3	13.7	16.4	11.0
Public administration, education, health, social services	11.5	14.5	14.4	15.1	16.8	5.4
Personal services	4.3	4.5	6.2	7.5	8.8	4.5
Services total	*49*	*56*	*64*	*72*	*80*	*31*
Total	*100.0*	*100.0*	*100.0*	*100.0*	*100.0*	
			Median Log Wage			
Utilities, agriculture	8.50	8.85	9.11	9.32	9.48	0.98
Manufacturing	8.28	8.54	8.93	9.10	9.32	1.03
Construction	8.71	8.78	9.11	9.16	9.22	0.51
Wholesale, retail, hotels/restaurants	8.50	8.70	8.93	8.99	9.11	0.61
Import/export	8.66	8.85	9.19	9.35	9.44	0.78
Transport, storage, and communication	8.79	8.85	9.11	9.21	9.27	0.48
Financing, insurance, real estate, business services	8.63	8.91	9.26	9.39	9.56	0.93
Public administration, education, health, social services	8.79	9.03	9.30	9.44	9.65	0.86
Personal services	8.28	8.39	8.49	8.23	8.25	−0.03
			Mean Log Wage			
Utilities, agriculture	8.59	8.73	9.16	9.38	9.54	0.95
Manufacturing	8.36	8.56	8.92	9.16	9.41	1.05
Construction	8.70	8.76	9.08	9.17	9.32	0.61
Wholesale, retail, hotels/restaurants	8.57	8.75	9.01	9.07	9.16	0.59
Import/export	8.80	9.03	9.30	9.44	9.52	0.72
Transport, storage, and communication	8.75	8.90	9.12	9.23	9.38	0.63
Financing, insurance, real estate, business services	8.76	9.04	9.38	9.50	9.64	0.88
Public administration, education, health, social services	8.89	9.13	9.33	9.53	9.67	0.79
Personal services	8.31	8.44	8.64	8.54	8.51	0.19
			Standard Deviation of Log Wages *(multiplied by 100)*			
Utilities, agriculture	69.7	74.8	68.9	71.1	77.3	7.6
Manufacturing	51.0	55.3	58.4	63.3	65.4	14.4
Construction	52.0	58.8	57.8	58.1	55.1	3.1
Wholesale, retail, hotels/restaurants	55.3	53.7	55.8	56.8	58.7	3.3
Import/export	65.7	63.8	61.9	64.3	65.1	−0.6
Transport, storage, and communication	45.9	48.2	50.6	55.6	59.3	13.4
Financing, insurance, real estate, business services	59.8	63.0	69.4	73.2	74.3	14.5
Public administration, education, health, social services	64.9	68.5	72.2	69.3	78.4	13.5
Personal services	45.3	49.6	48.8	49.4	50.7	5.3

Sources: Hong Kong SAR Census data; and IMF staff estimates.

has been much more pronounced in Hong Kong SAR.

The median monthly wage increased in all sectors, although at different rates. Wage gains are the lowest in the construction, wholesale and retail trade, transport, storage, and communications sectors. The relative share of low-skilled occupations in these sectors is large, suggesting that wage rises have been more moderate among low-skilled workers. Wage increases in manufacturing have been larger than in any other sector, suggesting that the downsizing of labor in that sector was mostly among low-skilled workers. This is consistent with studies noting that the stages of manufacturing remaining in Hong Kong SAR are

Table 6.3. Employed Men and Women: Employment and Wages, by Education

	1981	1986	1991	1996	2001	Change, 1981–2001
	Average Years of Education					
All employed	7.5	8.5	9.3	10.1	10.8	3.2
Men	7.7	8.5	9.1	9.9	10.6	2.9
Women	7.3	8.5	9.5	10.5	11.0	3.7
	Share in Total Employment (percent)					
Primary and no formal	47	36	27	20	16	−30.2
Lower-secondary	19	19	20	20	20	0.9
Upper-secondary	27	33	38	40	42	14.9
Postsecondary	4	6	7	6	5	1.5
Tertiary	4	6	7	13	17	13.0
	Median Log Wage					
Primary and no formal	8.4	8.5	8.8	8.9	9.0	0.60
Lower-secondary	8.5	8.7	8.9	9.0	9.1	0.61
Upper-secondary	8.6	8.8	9.1	9.2	9.3	0.70
Postsecondary	9.1	9.2	9.5	9.5	9.8	0.67
Tertiary	9.4	9.6	9.8	9.9	10.0	0.54
	Standard Deviation of Log Wages (multiplied by 100)					
Primary and no formal	50.3	52.1	49.7	52.2	54.8	4.5
Lower-secondary	49.2	48.7	49.7	50.9	53.7	4.5
Upper-secondary	55.3	55.9	56.5	58.6	64.5	9.2
Postsecondary	62.3	66.6	64.8	66.6	71.0	8.7
Tertiary	73.9	80.1	85.2	84.5	85.0	11.0

Sources: Hong Kong SAR Census; and IMF staff estimates.

increasingly concentrated in sophisticated, high-value-added managerial and administrative services.

The average educational level of the workforce has risen at a rapid rate over the sample period (Table 6.3). Workers with a primary education or less declined from 47 percent to 16 percent of all employees, and the share of workers with a tertiary education quadrupled. The Hong Kong SAR authorities introduced compulsory primary and lower-secondary education in the early 1970s, which can partially account for the increase in the average education level. Median wage increases have been the highest for people with upper-secondary and post-secondary education, supporting the conjecture that wage increases have been higher for the more skilled.

Table 6.4 shows the skill intensity of different sectors, measured by the share of workers with upper-secondary education or more. Finance, insurance, real estate, and business services is the most skill-intensive sector, and the share of skilled workers (see the center panel of Table 6.4) has remained constant over time. Among the major sectors, skill upgrading has been most significant in manufacturing.[6] The wage premium for workers with higher education has increased fastest in the sectors that produce or distribute tradable goods—manufacturing, transportation, and storage—suggesting that increased international trade and specialization in the production chain have benefited those with higher education.

Changes in Overall Wage Inequality

Wage inequality has risen substantially over the period, largely owing to rapid increases at the highest deciles of the income distribution. Table 6.5

---

[6]Personal services, which has registered the largest increase in the share of highly educated labor, is a sector with a large and growing share of immigrant labor, which commands very low wages independent of educational qualifications. Total employment in utilities and agriculture is very small, and developments in this sector are just shown for completeness.

Table 6.4. Education Attainment and Education Wage Premium, by Industry

	1981	1986	1991	1996	2001	Change, 1981–2001
	Average Years of Education, by Industry					
Utilities, agriculture	5.0	6.6	7.9	8.9	9.3	4.3
Manufacturing	7.0	7.7	8.4	9.5	10.4	3.4
Construction	6.6	7.6	7.9	8.4	8.6	1.9
Wholesale, retail, hotels/restaurants	6.7	7.6	8.4	9.0	9.4	2.6
Import/export	10.7	11.2	11.4	11.8	11.9	1.2
Transport, storage, and communication	7.8	8.3	8.9	9.5	10.1	2.3
Financing, insurance, real estate, business services	11.1	11.3	11.5	11.9	12.7	1.6
Public administration, education, health, social services	9.8	10.4	10.7	11.4	11.9	2.1
Personal services	5.8	8.3	9.5	10.3	10.8	5.0
Full sample	*7.5*	*8.5*	*9.3*	*10.1*	*10.8*	*3.2*
	Share of Workers with More Than 9 Years of Education, by Industry (percent)					
Utilities, agriculture	18	32	38	45	52	33.1
Manufacturing	24	33	40	52	60	35.5
Construction	22	32	31	35	35	13.0
Wholesale, retail, hotels/restaurants	27	36	41	45	49	21.6
Import/export	78	84	85	86	81	3.8
Transport, storage, and communication	37	42	48	52	56	19.3
Financing, insurance, real estate, business services	84	84	83	83	84	0.2
Public administration, education, health, social services	62	67	72	74	73	11.2
Personal services	21	45	55	63	67	46.5
Full sample	*35*	*45*	*53*	*60*	*64*	*29.4*
Correlation between changes in industry employment shares and changes in share of skilled workers		−0.31	−0.66	−0.94	−0.63	
	Skilled-Wage Premium, by Industry[1]					
Utilities, agriculture	3.6	7.2	8.9	8.1	11.8	8.2
Manufacturing	4.3	5.3	6.9	9.0	9.2	4.9
Construction	5.6	7.1	7.2	8.0	6.2	0.6
Wholesale, retail, hotels/restaurants	4.7	5.0	6.0	6.8	7.2	2.5
Import/export	8.9	7.8	9.2	9.2	9.9	0.9
Transport, storage, and communication	4.4	6.4	6.3	8.7	9.1	4.8
Financing, insurance, real estate, business services	10.4	11.8	12.7	13.1	12.7	2.3
Public administration, education, health, social services	9.0	10.8	12.2	11.6	12.8	3.8
Personal services	2.5	1.6	1.9	0.7	−0.2	−2.7
Full sample	*6.2*	*7.9*	*8.8*	*9.7*	*10.0*	*3.8*

Sources: Hong Kong SAR Census; and IMF staff estimates.

[1]The estimated skilled-wage premium is the coefficient on years of education in a regression of log wages on years of education, gender, experience, experience squared, and recent immigrant status.

contains different summary measures of wage dispersion—the standard deviation, the coefficient of variation, the Gini coefficient, and percentile differentials. Most measures indicate a steady increase. (One exception is the subperiod 1986 to 1991, when inequality among women declined slightly according to the first two measures.) The 90/10 percentile differential shows that the dispersion of wages increased sharply during the 1990s. By contrast, relative wages below the median (50/10 percentile differential) have remained unchanged for men and have risen for women only in the second half of the sample period. The increase in the 75/25 percentile

diferential is also very modest for men. These statistics suggest that the increase in overall wage inequality has come mostly from rising wages at the top of the distribution, while relative wages in the lower half of the distribution have remained largely unchanged. By these measures, wage inequality in Hong Kong SAR has grown much faster than in, for example, the United Kingdom (Table 6.6).[7]

---

[7]As has been well documented in the literature, 1980–98 was a period of rapid increase in wage inequality in the United Kingdom (see Prasad, 2002 and the references therein).

Table 6.5. Measures of Wage Inequality, 1981–2001

	1981	1986	1991	1996	2001	Change, 1981–2001
Standard deviation	0.58	0.62	0.64	0.68	0.73	0.15
Men	0.55	0.60	0.64	0.67	0.69	0.14
Women	0.55	0.60	0.59	0.66	0.73	0.19
Coefficient of variation *10	0.68	0.71	0.70	0.74	0.78	0.10
Men	0.64	0.68	0.69	0.71	0.72	0.09
Women	0.66	0.70	0.67	0.73	0.80	0.14
Gini coefficient	0.34	0.36	0.38	0.41	0.43	
Men	0.33	0.36	0.38	0.40	0.41	
Women	0.32	0.35	0.36	0.39	0.43	
			Wage Percentile Differentials			
All workers						
p90/p10	1.4	1.5	1.4	1.8	1.9	0.50
p90/p50	0.8	0.8	0.8	1.0	1.0	0.28
p50/p10	0.6	0.6	0.6	0.8	0.8	0.22
p75/p25	0.6	0.7	0.7	0.8	0.9	0.31
Men						
p90/p10	1.3	1.4	1.5	1.6	1.7	0.45
p90/p50	0.7	0.8	0.9	1.0	1.1	0.35
p50/p10	0.5	0.6	0.6	0.6	0.6	0.10
p75/p25	0.6	0.6	0.7	0.8	0.9	0.24
Women						
p90/p10	1.3	1.5	1.5	1.7	2.0	0.66
p90/p50	0.7	0.9	0.9	0.9	1.1	0.33
p50/p10	0.6	0.6	0.6	0.8	0.9	0.33
p75/p25	0.5	0.6	0.7	0.9	1.0	0.49

Sources: Hong Kong SAR Census; and IMF staff estimates.
Notes: The wage variable is the logarithm of real monthly wages. The letter "p" denotes percentile—for example, "p90" denotes the ninetieth percentile.

The widening of income disparity in Hong Kong SAR has been accompanied by rising real wages at all deciles of the distribution (Figure 6.2). Although wage growth has been higher at the top percentiles,

Table 6.6. Change in Log Wage Differentials, by Percentile

All Workers	Hong Kong SAR, 1981–2001	United Kingdom,[1] 1980–98
90–10	0.50	0.25
90–50	0.28	0.16
50–10	0.22	0.09
75–25	0.31	0.17

Sources: For Hong Kong SAR data: Hong Kong SAR Census; and IMF staff estimates. For U.K. data: Prasad (2002).
[1] Log hourly wages.

cumulative real wage growth has been quite substantial even at the bottom half of the distribution. (An exception is the real wage growth for women at the bottom 25 percent during the low-growth period 1996–2001.) This is in contrast to the United States, where real wage growth in the lower deciles was negative in the 1980s and early 1990s, especially for males (see Freeman and Katz, 1994).

Changes in Inequality Between and Within Groups

The rise in overall wage inequality may reflect a change in the average wages received by different groups in a society (between groups) or an increase in the dispersion of wages within those groups. The population sample is divided into groups by education and by industry of employment to examine the relative contributions of these two factors to changes in inequality over time. The evolution of the 90/10 percentile differential by group suggests that inequal-

Figure 6.2. Real Wage Growth, by Decile

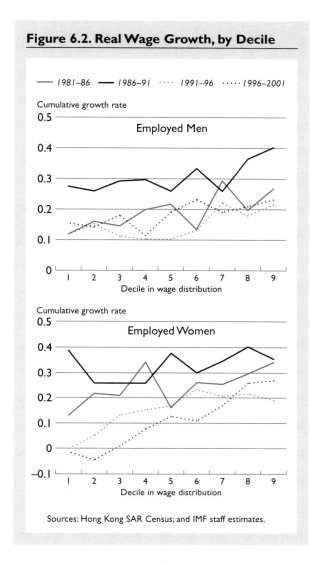

Sources: Hong Kong SAR Census; and IMF staff estimates.

Table 6.7. Measures of Residual Wage Inequality: Percentile Differentials

	1981	1986	1991	1996	2001	Change, 1981–2001
p90/p10	1.13	1.21	1.24	1.35	1.43	0.31
p90/p50	0.56	0.58	0.61	0.67	0.68	0.13
p50/p10	0.57	0.63	0.63	0.69	0.75	0.18

Sources: Hong Kong SAR Census; and IMF staff estimates.

Notes: Wage residuals are from regressions of log wages on dummies for education, experience, experience squared, marital status, and gender. The letter "p" denotes percentile—for example, "p90" denotes the ninetieth percentile.

group) inequality also accounts for close to three-quarters of the change in overall inequality.[10] Thus, the increase in inequality in Hong Kong SAR mostly reflects growing wage dispersion within education and industry groups. One interpretation of this large increase in inequality, after accounting for the effect of formal education and experience, is that the transformation of the economy from manufacturing to a trade-intermediary and financial center has increased the return to entrepreneurial ability.

Accounting for Evolution of Wage Inequality

Changes in Returns to Skills

A standard human-capital-regression framework is employed to study the evolution of returns to education for employed men and women, controlling for different personal characteristics. The logarithm of monthly wages is regressed on education dummies, labor-market experience, and dummies for marital status and recent immigrant status.[11] The results are reported in Table 6.8. The wage premium for upper-secondary education relative to lower-secondary education has risen from 17 percent in 1981 to 36 percent in 2001 for men. For postsecondary and tertiary education, the premiums were significantly

ity within both industry and education groups has risen.[8] An interesting observation is that inequality within the more educated groups is much greater than within less educated groups, suggesting that returns to unobserved skills (or ability) rise with education.

To examine changes in within-group inequality more formally, while controlling for between-group variation in observable skills, the residuals from a set of standard wage regressions are examined (Table 6.7).[9] This analysis indicates that within-group inequality accounts for more than three-quarters of total inequality. The change in residual (within-

---

[8]The detailed results for industry groups and education-attainment groups are reported in IMF (2002).

[9]Log wages are regressed on years of experience; experience squared; and dummies for education, gender, and marital status.

---

[10]Separate regressions of wages on a group of education dummies, industry dummies, and gender dummies were estimated. The regression on education dummies reduced the residual inequality the most, relative to overall wage inequality, indicating that inequality between education categories is the largest contributor to between-group inequality.

[11]Potential labor-market experience has been imputed from the individual's age and approximate years of education, based on educational attainment. A second-order polynomial of this variable is included in the regressions.

Table 6.8. Returns to Education and Experience Based on Human-Capital Equations

	Men					Women				
	1981	1986	1991	1996	2001	1981	1986	1991	1996	2001
					Education Premiums[1]					
Education level										
Upper-secondary/crafts	1.17	1.26	1.28	1.31	1.36	1.40	1.41	1.45	1.47	1.42
Postsecondary/technical institute	1.67	1.90	1.94	1.97	2.15	2.30	2.30	2.20	2.09	2.33
Tertiary	2.16	2.58	2.87	2.84	3.02	2.84	2.88	2.59	2.64	2.77
					Returns to Experience[2]					
Potential experience level										
5 years	2.7	3.7	3.7	4.2	4.9	1.8	3.1	2.7	2.6	3.6
15 years	1.2	1.8	1.8	2.1	2.6	0.8	1.5	1.1	1.1	1.8
25 years	−0.3	0.0	−0.1	0.1	0.2	−0.3	0.0	−0.4	−0.3	−0.1

Sources: Hong Kong SAR Census; and IMF staff estimates.

Note: The results are based on a regression of log wages on years of experience, years of experience squared, and dummies for education, marital status, and recent immigration status. The detailed results were reported in IMF (2002).

[1]The premiums are relative to lower-secondary education (exponent of the ordinary-least-squares (OLS) coefficients).

[2]Returns to experience are evaluated at specific experience levels.

higher and have increased faster over the period. The levels of the premiums are at the upper range of those typically found in other advanced economies, although differences in the definition of education variables make cross-country comparisons difficult. The increase in the premiums has also been very rapid. This happened despite the significant increase in workers' average education, which implies that the increase in demand for more educated workers has persistently outpaced the increase in supply.

The returns to experience also have increased over time. One possible explanation is that practical experience has become more valuable during the period of structural change. An alternative, or complementary, explanation could be that any downward wage adjustments have been concentrated among new entrants in the labor market.

Changes in Relative Wages Versus Changes in Relative Unemployment

It is often argued that labor market rigidities in continental Europe have constrained relative wage changes, and adjustment to structural shifts has taken place through higher unemployment for the unskilled.[12] In the United States and the United Kingdom, which have relatively flexible labor markets, the adjustment has been accomplished mostly through a decline in relative wages and less so through differential unemployment rates. Hong

Kong SAR's labor market is practically free of institutional constraints—there are no minimum wages and no unemployment insurance; less than 2 percent of the labor force is unionized; income taxes are low; and labor legislation is very limited. Therefore, one would expect the adjustment process to be similar to that in the United States.

In the period of rapid economic growth (before 1997), unemployment among both skilled and unskilled workers was very low (Figure 6.3). This

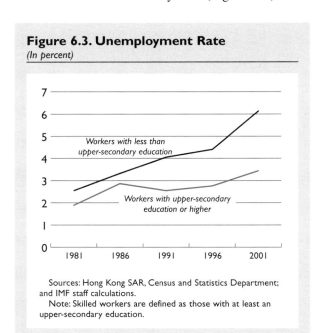

Figure 6.3. Unemployment Rate
(In percent)

Sources: Hong Kong SAR, Census and Statistics Department; and IMF staff calculations.

Note: Skilled workers are defined as those with at least an upper-secondary education.

---

[12]See Davis (1998). Prasad (2004) reviews the literature and does a case study of the German labor market.

Table 6.9. Decomposition of Increase in Share of Skilled Workers
(In percent)

| | Employment | | | | | |
| | Manufacturing | | | Nonmanufacturing | | |
	Between	Within	Total	Between	Within	Total
1981–86	0.24	8.00	8.23	2.28	8.00	10.28
1986–91	0.29	7.12	7.41	1.92	3.81	5.73
1991–96	0.80	11.36	12.17	0.80	3.03	3.82
1996–2001	0.32	7.40	7.72	1.41	1.74	3.15
	Wage Bill					
1981–86	0.28	9.10	9.38	2.24	9.18	11.41
1986–91	0.28	10.74	11.02	1.54	4.35	5.89
1991–96	0.86	11.04	11.90	0.52	3.43	3.95
1996–2001	0.11	5.86	5.97	1.20	2.20	3.40

Sources: Hong Kong SAR Census; and IMF staff estimates.

Notes: Skilled workers are defined as those with more than nine years of education. All manufacturing industries were grouped into six categories.

supports the hypothesis that flexible labor markets in Hong Kong SAR have allowed shifts in the relative demand for skilled labor to be accommodated through relative wage changes. However, during the prolonged cyclical downturn since 1997, unemployment among unskilled workers has increased much faster than among skilled workers. This was a period of significant deflation, and it is possible that partial downward nominal rigidity of wages has prevented full adjustment through changes in the price of labor.

Effects of Sectoral Shifts

Both skill-biased technical change and increased outsourcing to the mainland could have contributed to the increase in demand for skilled workers within industries. One way to differentiate between these explanations is to compare the changes in relative demand for skilled workers in industries that experienced a greater degree of outsourcing to changes in relative demand in industries with less outsourcing. Assuming that skill-biased technological change has been similar for all sectors, such a comparison would reveal whether outsourcing has contributed to the increase in wage inequality.[13] A

standard decomposition of the growth of the share of skilled employment can be used to illustrate the importance of relative demand shifts within industries versus the reallocation of labor to industries with a higher share of skilled workers as follows:

$$\Delta E_{jt} = \sum_i (\Delta E_{it} \alpha_{jt}) + \sum_i (\Delta \alpha_{jit} E_i), \quad (1)$$

where the index i denotes industries; j denotes the type of worker (skilled or unskilled); $\alpha_{jit} = E_{jit}/E_{it}$ is the group j share of employment in industry i in year t; and $E_i = (E_{it} + E_{it-1})/2$. The first term of equation (1) is the change in the aggregate share of skilled workers attributable to changes in employment shares *between industries* that use different proportions of skilled workers. The second term captures *within-industry* increases in the share of skilled workers. A similar decomposition is performed to analyze changes in the aggregate-wage-bill share of skilled workers.[14]

Table 6.9 presents the decomposition of the growth in the share of skilled employment in total employment and the decomposition of the skilled-wage-bill share for all manufacturing and nonmanufacturing industries. Between 1986 and 2001, the increase in the share of skilled employment has been much greater in manufacturing than in nonmanufacturing industries. The within-industry component of the increase in skilled employment accounts for

[13]Acemoglu (2003) suggests that it may be difficult to differentiate empirically between these two explanations, since they may both be present and reinforce each other. For example, more active international trade in certain sectors may induce sector-specific, skill-biased technological change. The magnitude of employment shifts in Hong Kong SAR suggests, however, that the production-outsourcing effect dominates possible technological-change effects.

[14]Hsieh and Woo (2000) uses the same technique to isolate the effect of outsourcing. The analysis in this section finds that their results hold when the time period is extended to 2001.

practically all of the increase for the manufacturing industries. The between-industry component is much more significant for the nonmanufacturing industries, which supports the conjecture that outsourcing is linked to greater-than-average within-industry skill upgrading.

Conclusions

This section finds that between 1981 and 2001, real wages in Hong Kong SAR have increased substantially across the wage distribution while wage disparity has risen. Wage inequality within industry groups has increased as industry structures have shifted toward specialization in higher-value-added services. Wage premiums for higher education are large and have generally increased over the period despite an increase in the supply of educated workers, pointing to a significant shift in the relative demand for educated labor. Earnings inequality is greater among more educated groups and has increased over time, suggesting that returns to unobservable skills have increased at higher levels of education.

Both outsourcing and skill-biased technological change could have led to the observed within-industry skill upgrading and increase in skill premiums. It was not the goal of this section to determine the relative contribution of these two influences. The fact that within-industry relative demand shifts were more significant in manufacturing than in other industries, however, supports the conjecture that outsourcing has been an important cause of the observed changes.

The empirical analysis suggests that policies to increase the skill level of the labor force would be most effective in addressing structural imbalances in the labor market. Enrollment in upper- and postsecondary education and government spending on education are much lower in Hong Kong SAR than in OECD countries. Continuing economic integration with the mainland would likely lead to a further increase in the relative demand for skilled labor and rising relative returns to education and other skills. An increase in the education level of the labor force, by itself, may not make the distribution of income more equal, but it will increase equality of opportunity and contribute to sustainable economic growth, which historically has led to improvement of living standards even for the poorest.

VII Financial Market Developments

William Lee and Ida Liu

Hong Kong SAR is a leading international financial center with a resilient and fundamentally strong network of financial institutions and markets. Its extensive and deepening links with the mainland, large banking sector, well-capitalized stock market, and active foreign exchange markets enable it to compete effectively with other regional financial centers. Hong Kong SAR's strong legal framework, a world-class regulatory and supervisory apparatus, and leading-edge financial infrastructure are sources of stability that attract global investors and businesses. This section reviews these and other advantages that have allowed the financial system to successfully confront and overcome a number of shocks and crises over the years while meeting new challenges resulting from advances in information technology and rapidly changing financial practices.[1]

An International Financial Center

As one of the most open economies in the Asia-Pacific region, Hong Kong SAR has developed into a leading international financial center whose outward investment orientation compares favorably with that of other centers (Table 7.1). This orientation is evident from Hong Kong SAR's unusually large international investment positions; as a share of GDP, holdings of foreign assets and liabilities are several times larger than those of other existing or prospective regional financial centers (Table 7.2). Recent capital-account transactions among regional financial centers show that direct investment and bank flows (accounting for most of the "other investment flows" category) play a key role in directing capital into Hong Kong SAR.

Most globally important financial institutions in the banking, insurance, and securities businesses maintain their regional headquarters or some other presence in Hong Kong SAR for managing funds and as a gateway for promoting financial products to domestic and regional investors, especially those on the mainland.[2] Compared with regional financial centers, Hong Kong SAR's banking system, stock market, and foreign exchange market rank third in the Asia-Pacific region when measured by total assets, market capitalization, and turnover. The growth of the banking sector and the deepening of liquidity in financial markets reflect the importance of a strategic geographic location, a liberal regime toward foreign bank and equity ownership, and an absence of controls on cross-border goods and financial flows for residents and nonresidents.

Financial Intermediation Mainly Through Banks

The financial sector is dominated by institutions that are active in banking and the securities business (Table 7.3). These large banking institutions are major participants in the interbank market, serve as market makers in important exchange-traded contracts and the over-the-counter (OTC) market, and are important agents in underwriting and placing debt securities. Compared with other international financial centers, the ratio of deposits to GDP of Hong Kong SAR's banks is among the highest, which illustrates the importance of banks in channeling domestic savings into investments. Moreover, syndicated loan volume in Hong Kong SAR is the second largest in Asia, which is consistent with the view that intermediation is performed largely by banks rather than through direct issuance of market instruments. Although there are many banks, the banking system is highly concentrated and accounts for two-thirds of the financial system's total assets.[3] Reflecting the international character of Hong Kong SAR's banking system, several of the largest are for-

---

[1]This chapter draws from material in the *Hong Kong SAR Yearbook 2001* and the IMF's Financial System Stability Assessment report for Hong Kong SAR (International Monetary Fund, 2003).

[2]At the end of 2001, there were 133 foreign-owned banks in Hong Kong SAR, of which 76 were among the world's top 100 banks in terms of total assets.

[3]As a result of this concentration, interest margins are high by developed-country standards, which has contributed to the sector's track record of high returns on assets and equity.

Table 7.1. Comparative Standing Among International Financial Centers, 2001[1]

	Asia-Pacific Region						Luxembourg	Zurich (Switzerland)	London (United Kingdom)	New York (United States)
	Hong Kong SAR	Sydney (Australia)	Shanghai (Mainland of China)	Tokyo (Japan)	Seoul (Korea)	Singapore				
Economies of Scale and Scope (billion U.S. dollars)										
Deposit-money banks' total assets	789	379	1,947	6,473	461	191	573	876	4,183	9,435
Stock-market capitalization[2]	498	776	520	1,578	197	109	400	496	1,800	10,410
Domestic bonds outstanding[3]	44	170	368	5,817	293	52	...	159	921	15,290
Spot foreign exchange market turnover (daily average)	19	13	...	37	6	34	4	23	151	104
Derivatives' foreign exchange market turnover (daily average)	49	39	...	110	4	66	9	47	353	150
OTC single-currency interest rate derivatives turnover (daily average)	3	10	...	16	8	3	4	10	238	116
Consolidated international claims of reporting banks on country	100	44	27	97	32	55	99	69	499	787
International Economic Links										
Exports of goods and services as percentage of GDP	141	22	...	10	43	...	...	44	27	10
Number of domestic banks ranked in world's top 1,000	13	9	15	121	14	3	7	36	36	228
Deposit-money banks' foreign assets as percentage of total assets[4]	51	8	6	12	6	32	...	51	53	5
Credibility and Creditworthiness										
International reserves (billion U.S. dollars)	111	18	219	401	104	76	...	36	38	70
Deposit-money banks' foreign liabilities as percentage of total liabilities[5]	33	26	2	9	5	33	...	47	53	7
Memorandum item:										
Deposit-to-loan ratio (in percent)	154	75	109	108	86	92	...	77	81	...

Source: IMF, 2003, People's Republic of China–Hong Kong Special Administrative Region: Financial System Stability Assessment (Washington).

Note: OTC denotes over the counter.

[1] Data are for the economies in which the respective international financial centers are located.
[2] Main Board for Hong Kong SAR.
[3] For Hong Kong SAR, Hong Kong dollar debt instruments other than Exchange Fund bills and notes.
[4] Foreign assets refer to total external claims.
[5] Foreign liabilities refer to total external liabilities.

Table 7.2. Comparison of International Investment Positions Among Existing and Emerging Regional Financial Centers (RFCs), 2002

	Assets	Liabilities	Gross Position	Percent of GDP	Net Position	Percent of GDP
		(billion U.S. dollars)			*(billion U.S. dollars)*	
Existing RFCs						
Hong Kong SAR[1]	1,071	805	1,876	1,143.9	265	161.6
Japan	2,918	1,520	4,438	107.2	1,398	33.8
Singapore	373	329	702	807.2	43	49.4
Australia	255	466	721	180.9	211	52.9
Emerging RFCs						
Republic of Korea[1]	185	250	435	101.8	65	15.2
Thailand	58	105	163	128.9	47	37.2

Sources: CEIC Data Co., Ltd.; Bank of Korea; Australia Statistics Bureau; and Singapore Statistics Bureau.
[1]Figures as of the end of 2001.

eign banks that have large shares of the deposit base and the market for many bank products.

In recent years, bank lending has been shrinking, and total assets have declined by 27 percent since 1997. In addition to the effects of industry consolidation, offshore banking activities have declined as euro-yen loans have diminished because of changes in Japanese tax treatment of such loans. Although bank profits and liquidity have historically been high by international standards, the recent global slowdown has reduced domestic lending and increased pressure on industry profits.[4] Increasingly, competition and advances in technology have spurred banks, even the smaller ones, to enter the securities and insurance businesses.

Peer assessments by bank regulators and supervisors have noted that the banking system remains sound and well run despite the strains it has been under recently (see Box 7.1). Factors supporting the well-run banking sector include (1) high capital-adequacy ratios; (2) strong supervisory and regulatory practices; (3) a low level of classified loans; (4) small direct exchange rate risk, reflecting small open positions in foreign exchange; and (5) a track record of resilience to external shocks. Stress tests suggest that the banking system would generally be able to withstand a combination of further declines in property prices, increases in classified loans, and changes in interest rates that are comparable to those that occurred during the turbulent 1997–98 period.

Looking forward, the main challenges to the banking industry and regulatory and supervisory policy are likely to emerge from (1) the global changes in financial practices that are reshaping the financial sector through industry mergers and acquisitions, and cross-market links from new financial products; and (2) increased economic integration with the mainland of China, which will boost cross-border trade and investment flows, encourage Hong Kong SAR banks to open new branches and subsidiaries on the mainland, and require harmonization of regulatory and supervisory policies and practices with the mainland.[5]

More immediate challenges and risks stem from the global and domestic weakening in economic activity since 2000. Bank lending has been noticeably reduced, as have bank profits, notwithstanding industry efforts to expand the array of bank products and services. In particular, the decline in property prices has increased the number and value of mortgages that exceed the value of the underlying property, creating negative equity. Recent estimates by the Hong Kong Monetary Authority (HKMA) place about a quarter of residential mortgages in a deep negative-equity position (where the mortgage exceeds the property value by 50 percent or more). In this respect, large global banks are often seen as sources of stability for the system, while small banks may be more exposed to such domestic sources of risk and could be a source of reputation risk to the banking system.

---

[4]Domestic bank lending declined by 15 percent between 1997 and 2002 as bank holdings of securities and other investments almost doubled.

[5]The steps taken by the Hong Kong SAR authorities to improve the supervisory and regulatory frameworks in response to the recommendations of the Financial Sector Assessment Program carried out by the IMF staff are described in Box 7.2.

Table 7.3. Structure of Financial System, 1997–2002

	Number of Institutions				Total Assets (billion U.S. dollars)				Percentage of Total Assets		Percentage of GDP	
	Dec. 97	Dec. 99	Dec. 01	Jun. 02	Dec. 97	Dec. 99	Dec. 01	Jun. 02	Dec. 97	Dec. 01	Dec. 97	Dec. 01
Authorized (deposit-taking) institutions	361	285	250	229	1,076.6	869.8	789.0	780.6	84.3	66.6	624.5	481.2
Licensed banks	180	156	147	133	1,011.1	828.9	753.6	746.2	79.1	63.7	586.5	459.6
Incorporated in Hong Kong SAR	31	31	29	27	254.3	285.7	381.4	376.3	19.9	32.2	147.5	232.6
Incorporated outside Hong Kong SAR	149	125	118	106	756.8	543.3	372.2	369.9	59.2	31.4	439.0	227.0
Restricted license banks	66	58	49	48	45.5	31.7	28.7	28.4	3.6	2.4	26.4	17.5
Deposit-taking companies	115	71	54	48	20.0	9.2	6.6	6.0	1.6	0.6	11.6	4.1
Institutional investors	20,080	21,191	12,635	2,270	171.2	348.1	345.7	277.3	13.4	29.2	100.1	213.6
Insurance companies	215	207	204	203	25.4	31.2	35.0	...	2.0	3.0	14.8	21.6
General and composite insurance	170	165	159	155	2.5	2.1	2.3	...	0.2	0.2	1.5	1.4
Pure long-term insurance	45	42	45	48	22.9	29.0	32.7	...	1.8	2.8	13.4	20.2
Collective investment schemes	19,865	20,984	12,431	2,067	145.9	316.9	310.7	277.3	11.4	26.2	85.3	191.9
Unit trusts and mutual funds	1,472	1,577	1,893	1,900	132.4	298.9	285.2	277.3	10.4	24.1	77.4	176.2
Investment-linked assurance schemes	60	63	98	109	...	...	...	...	...	...	...	...
Pooled retirement funds	18,259	19,285	9,809	...	13.5	18.1	20.9	...	1.1	1.8	7.9	12.9
Provident schemes, constituent funds, and pooled investment funds	...	...	579	58	...	...	4.6	...	...	0.0	...	2.9
Others	74	59	52	58	...	...	...	...	...	...	...	...
Registered intermediaries	1,659	1,601	1,689	1,695	29.9	36.4	49.2	21.1	2.3	4.2	17.5	30.4
Securities intermediaries	1,346	1,297	1,397	1,402	29.5	36.0	36.9	19.3	2.3	3.1	17.2	22.8
Dealers[1]	707	695	720	718	14.1	14.1	14.6	18.3	1.1	1.2	8.2	9.0
Advisers	639	602	669	676	15.4	21.9	21.3	...	1.2	1.8	9.0	13.1
Margin financiers	...	...	8	8	...	...	1.0	1.0	...	0.1	...	0.6
Commodities intermediaries	292	288	281	283	0.1	0.1	12.1	1.5	0.0	1.0	0.1	7.4
Dealers[1]	162	160	155	155	0.1	0.1	1.5	1.5	0.0	0.1	0.1	1.0
Advisers	130	128	126	128	0.0	0.0	10.5	0.0	0.0	0.9	0.0	6.5
Leveraged foreign exchange traders[2]	21	16	11	10	0.3	0.3	0.3	0.3	0.0	0.0	0.1	0.2
Other financial intermediaries[3]	1,139	1,035	865	835	0.1	1.8	8.5	0.0	0.0	0.7	0.1	5.2
Hong Kong Mortgage Corporation	1	...	1	1	0.1	1.8	3.0	...	0.0	0.3	0.1	1.8
Moneylenders	1,138	1,034	864	834	...	...	5.5	...	...	0.5	...	3.4
Total financial system	22,100	23,077	14,574	4,194	1,277.7	1,254.3	1,183.9	1,079.1	100.0	100.0	747.2	731.2
Memorandum items:												
Local representative offices of foreign banks	159	127	111	102					...	...	...	...
Companies listed on stock market[4]	658	708	867	924	410.6	606.1	498.1	486.1	...	...	240.1	307.7

Source: IMF, 2003, People's Republic of China—Hong Kong Special Administrative Region: Financial System Stability Assessment (Washington).

[1] Dealers who also have adviser licenses are included here and eliminated from the adviser category.

[2] Leveraged foreign exchange traders are not required to report total assets in their monthly financial returns. Total liquid assets are shown as a proxy for total assets.

[3] Finance, hire-purchase, and leasing companies; comprehensive data on them are not available, however.

[4] Number of listed companies and market capitalization of Hong Kong SAR cash market (Main Board) in billion U.S. dollars.

Box 7.1. Findings of Financial Sector Assessment Program

Overall, the assessment confirms that the Hong Kong SAR financial system is robust and fundamentally sound. Hong Kong SAR's financial system has shown resilience in the midst of recent international financial crises and during the domestic cyclical downturn. Although some improvements in financial sector supervision and regulatory governance arrangements are recommended, no immediate issues of systemic instability are apparent.

Financial markets are well developed, liquid, and efficient. The banking system, in particular, is well capitalized and profitable. Weak demand for corporate loans and declining interest rate margins on mortgage loans, however, are driving banks, even smaller ones, to expand into investment banking, securities brokerage, insurance brokerage, and asset-management services. Linkages of the banking sector with the capital markets and insurance sectors are growing, motivating enhanced supervisory coordination among regulators of the banking, insurance, and securities industries. This also highlights the need to strengthen legislation related to regulatory and insolvency procedures for financial conglomerates. The recently established Mandatory Provident Fund will help to develop the local capital market but faces structural challenges stemming from its low current returns and a projected income-replacement rate that is within international norms but depends on maintaining the present contribution rates, long service in the system, and nonwithdrawal of funds upon separation.

The assessment finds that the necessary regulatory infrastructure is in place to support the efficient functioning of financial markets. Nevertheless, governance of the securities settlement system (SSS) would benefit from greater stakeholder participation. As with the SSS for securities transfer, the payment system would also benefit from approval of pending legislation to ensure finality of settlements in funds transfer. In the area of corporate governance, fostering wider shareholder participation would help ensure equitable treatment of minority shareholders, especially in view of the concentrated ownership structures. The report by the Expert Group to Review the Operation of the Securities and Futures Market Regulatory Structure, released in March 2003, has made a number of recommendations to strengthen the regulatory structure. The government broadly considers the recommendations to be appropriate and is currently reviewing them. It is also reviewing the feasibility of transferring the listing function from Hong Kong Exchanges and Clearing to the Securities and Futures Commission (SFC). Prompt approval of these proposed changes would clarify regulatory roles and strengthen enforcement in, and oversight of, the equities market. The

accounting and auditing professions and practices are adequate to support a market-based financial system; emphasis should be placed on improved corporate-disclosure requirements and enhanced disciplinary procedures in cases of professional misconduct.

The supervisory framework in Hong Kong SAR, which is well developed by international standards, is evolving rapidly from a regulatory compliance focus toward addressing prudential and market-conduct issues, and comprehensively assessing financial intermediaries' risk-management capabilities and contingency plans. Coordinated supervisory contingency planning, stress testing, and the use of early-warning indicators are welcome recent developments. The SFC and the Hong Kong Monetary Authority (HKMA) have developed effective information-sharing arrangements, including with foreign regulators and offshore centers. Oversight and regulation of the life insurance sector has been strengthened but may still pose some risks related to excessive supervisory reliance on actuaries and self-regulatory organizations. Data collection could be further improved to enable better assessment of market risk and profitability of the life-insurance sector.

The assessment recommends further strengthening of regulatory governance arrangements dealing with systemic and financial stability issues. Cross-sector and system-wide regulatory responsibilities can be better clarified and made public; the monitoring of factors affecting financial stability can be strengthened; and the collection of data on a system-wide basis can be improved. The transparency of institutional and policy frameworks for financial and systemic stability could be further enhanced by publishing the terms of reference of the high-level Council of Financial Regulators and by formalizing accountability and disclosure procedures in dealings between the Chief Executive of Hong Kong SAR and the Financial Secretary.

Hong Kong SAR has largely put in place a framework for anti-money laundering and combating the financing of terrorism that is in accordance with the Financial Action Task Force (FATF) recommendations. The banking, securities, and insurance authorities have issued guidelines on the prevention of money laundering since enactment of anti-money laundering legislation in 1989, and these have undergone a number of subsequent revisions. Recently, the authorities have issued for industry consultation proposed supplements aimed primarily at updating existing guidelines to reflect legislative changes and/or to conform with international standards set out by the Basel Committee on Banking Supervision and with certain recommendations currently under review by the FATF.

Financial Markets

Hong Kong SAR has the full range of financial markets: equity, debt, interbank, foreign exchange, and derivatives.

- The most important market for intermediation is the stock market, which has operated efficiently and has long provided a low-cost source of funds for listed companies. The Hong Kong

---

Box 7.2. Response of Hong Kong SAR Government to Recommendations of Financial Sector Assessment Program (FSAP)

Although the FSAP for Hong Kong SAR found the financial system to be robust and fundamentally sound, some improvements in financial sector supervision and regulatory governance arrangements were recommended. This box outlines actions taken to date by the Hong Kong SAR government in response to those recommendations. (FSAP recommendations appear in boldface italics; the authorities' actions appear in regular type.)

Further strengthen regulatory governance arrangements and improve the transparency of institutional and policy frameworks. The terms of reference of the Council of Financial Regulators and the Financial Stability Committee were published in late June 2003. At the same time, the responsibilities delegated to top finance officials, including the Financial Secretary and Secretary for Financial Services and the Treasury, were clarified, with policy formation and execution responsibilities clearly separated. A formal statement of monetary policy aims was also released, which made explicit that the operating mandate of the Hong Kong Monetary Authority (HKMA) is to maintain exchange rate stability. See *http://www.info.gov.hk/fstb/fsb/report/index.htm.*

Enhance cross-industry supervisory coordination. In September 2003, the HKMA and Office of the Commissioner of Insurance (OCI) signed a memorandum of understanding (MOU) outlining their respective responsibilities for regulating banks' insurance business. Under the MOU, the HKMA is responsible for the daily regulation of banks' insurance business. In cases of complaints of malpractice, the two regulators will share investigative work and take disciplinary action as needed.

Note: This box was prepared by Paul Gruenwald and Ida Liu.

Strengthen cross-border information-sharing mechanisms and regulatory arrangements, in particular with the mainland of China. The HKMA signed an MOU with the China Banking Regulatory Commission (CBRC) in late August 2003 to strengthen supervision of banks operating on both sides of the border. The MOU calls for the HKMA and the CBRC to share supervisory information on banks operating on the mainland and in Hong Kong SAR and to ensure that parent banks will exercise "adequate and effective" control over the operations of their cross-border branches and subsidiaries. The two regulators will also meet twice a year.

Improve corporate governance by fostering shareholder participation, ensuring equitable treatment of minority shareholders, improving the frequency and quality of reporting, and enhancing board oversight. The Standing Committee on Company Law Reform issued a consultation paper in June 2003 on the proposal to amend the Companies Ordinance to make it easier for investors to seek compensation for unfair connected transactions involving major shareholders. Other proposals in the consultation paper include adding statutory backing to listing rules, forcing companies to rotate their lead auditor partner every five years, and specifying the remuneration of individual directors. The consultation ended in September 2003.

Establish an independent legal basis for the OCI in order to bring Hong Kong SAR into line with international practice and improve oversight of the insurance industry. The Hong Kong SAR government finished its consultation at the end of June 2003 on the proposal to turn the OCI into a self-funded independent regulatory body. Opinion and views collected from the consultation are being examined by the Financial Services and Treasury Bureau.

SAR stock market's capitalization compares with that of Switzerland and accounts for more than 80 percent of the capital raised abroad by mainland companies. Funds raised in H-share and red-chip markets amounted to US$92.3 billion, more than 50 percent of the total funds raised in the Hong Kong SAR market during the last decade.[6]

- The size of the Hong Kong dollar debt market is small relative to the capitalization of the equities market, and, when measured relative to GDP, is

---

[6]H-shares are shares of mainland-incorporated companies listed in Hong Kong SAR, while the red chips are shares of Hong Kong SAR-incorporated companies with controlling stakes held by state-owned organizations of provincial/municipal authorities on the mainland.

about half the size of the debt market in Singapore (Table 7.4). The efficient intermediation by banks and the equities market has lowered the cost of capital from these sources to the point that domestic corporations have little need to raise funds through debt offerings. More recently, the low-interest-rate environment and high liquidity in bank balance sheets have prompted overseas borrowers, statutory bodies, and government-owned corporations to increase debt issuance.

- Since Hong Kong SAR is a bank-dominated international financial center, its interbank market provides an important source of liquidity from which international banks without deposit bases can obtain funding. Wholesale deposits are traded actively among local banks (in

Table 7.4. Relative Importance of Different Financing Channels in Selected Asian Economies, 2001

Country/ Economy	GDP (billion U.S. dollars)	Bank Loans (billion U.S. dollars)	(percent)	Stock Market Capitalization (billion U.S. dollars)	(percent)	Bond Market (billion U.S. dollars)	(percent)	Of Which: Public Sector Bonds (billion U.S. dollars)	(percent)	Private Sector Bonds (billion U.S. dollars)	(percent)
Hong Kong SAR	161.9	252.6	156.0	506.1	312.6	63.3	39.1	19.2	30.3	44.1	69.7
Indonesia	143.4	28.7	20.0	23.0	16.0	5.4	3.8	4.0	74.1	1.4	25.9
Korea, Rep. of	414.9	405.7	97.8	194.5	46.9	261.4	63.0	125.3	47.9	136.1	52.1
Malaysia	87.5	95.9	109.6	119.0	136.0	49.7	56.8	28.6	57.5	21.1	42.5
Philippines	70.6	25.1	35.6	21.2	30.0	3.2	4.5	2.1	65.6	1.1	34.4
Singapore	83.2	100.3	120.6	115.7	139.1	55.1	66.2	31.9	57.9	23.1	41.9
Taiwan Province of China	273.0	365.6	133.9	292.6	107.2	82.4	30.2	53.2	64.6	29.2	35.4
Thailand	115.4	85.4	74.0	35.9	31.1	42.6	36.9	30.4	71.4	12.2	28.6
Average	**168.7**	**169.9**	**100.7**	**163.5**	**96.9**	**70.4**	**41.7**	**36.8**	**52.3**	**33.5**	**47.6**
United States	10,208.1	7,587.5	74.3	13,923.4	136.4	17,118.0	167.7	10,010.8	58.5	7,107.2	41.5
United Kingdom	1,439.0	1,998.1	138.9	2,149.5	149.4	601.2	41.8	419.7	69.8	181.5	30.2
Japan	3,825.0	4,094.1	107.0	2,264.5	59.2	4,965.1	129.8	3,879.1	78.1	1,086.1	21.9
Average	**5,157.4**	**4,559.9**	**88.4**	**6,112.5**	**118.5**	**7,561.4**	**146.6**	**4,769.9**	**63.1**	**2,791.6**	**36.9**

Source: Hong Kong Monetary Authority, *Quarterly Bulletin*, March 2003.

Notes: (1) Bank loans are domestic credit extended to the private sector. All bank loan data, except for Taiwan Province of China, are reported in Line 32 of the IMF's *International Financial Statistics*. (2) All outstanding bond data are as of the end of 2001, except for Japan (end of March 2001); Indonesia, Malaysia, and the United Kingdom (end of 2000); and the Philippines (end of 1999). Data refer to local currency-denominated bonds. (3) Bond data for Hong Kong SAR, the Republic of Korea, Taiwan Province of China, the United States, the United Kingdom, and Japan are from central banks. The data for Indonesia, Malaysia, and the Philippines are from the International Finance Corporation (IFC) Bond Database. The data for Thailand are from the Thai Bond Dealing Center. The data for Singapore are estimated based on the Monetary Authority of Singapore and Thomson Financial Data. (4) Public sector refers to government bodies and quasi-government entities. (5) Private sector refers to nonpublic sector and includes financial institutions, corporations, and overseas institutions.

domestic currency), and between local and overseas institutions (usually in U.S. dollars). Interbank assets have declined by 23 percent in 2002–2003, mainly because of a reallocation away from interbank placements and toward market securities.

- Foreign exchange market trading has been active, with daily turnover equivalent to 41 percent of annual GDP, which compares with 35 percent in the United Kingdom. The latest triennial survey coordinated by the Bank for International Settlements (BIS) shows the daily average foreign exchange turnover in April 2001 to be US$66.8 billion, which represents 4 percent of the world's total transactions and makes Hong Kong SAR the world's seventh-largest foreign exchange market.
- Hong Kong SAR's derivatives market is among Asia's largest. Foreign exchange-related derivatives form the bulk of the trade in the derivatives market, although other forms of OTC instruments are also prevalent.

Taking advantage of the broad array of market instruments and funds from domestic and overseas investors, the fund-management industry in Hong Kong SAR has emphasized its international characteristics, both in terms of the presence of global fund managers and of authorized funds.[7] The growth of the Mandatory Provident Fund, the recently instituted retirement-saving vehicle, is expected to boost further the funds available for professional management and increase the demand for fixed-income and other market instruments.

The well-supervised securities markets face regulatory and supervisory challenges from global financial trends that could increase cross-market risks. As is occurring in other international financial centers, banks have been increasingly participating in securities market activities. Updated legislation (especially the Securities and Futures Ordinance) and increased cooperation and coordination between the Securities and Futures Commission and the HKMA should go a long way toward ensuring adequate surveillance and a level playing field for banks and brokers. As global investors have been demanding ever-higher standards of accounting disclosure and corporate governance, the Hong Kong SAR government has stepped up its commitment to improving

---

[7]Total assets under management by portfolio managers were HK$1.49 trillion (US$190.4 billion) at the end of 2002.

Table 7.5. China's Utilized Foreign Direct Investment (FDI), by Sources
(In millions of U.S. dollars)

	Total FDI	Total	Percent of Total	Hong Kong SAR	Percent of Total	Taiwan Province of China	Percent of Total	Japan	Percent of Total	Singapore	Percent of Total	Offshore Centers[1]	
												Total	Percent of Total
1994	33,767.0	26,311.4	77.9	19,665.4	58.2	3,391.0	10.0	2,075.3	6.1	1,179.6	3.5	...	...
1995	37,521.0	28,140.0	75.0	20,050.0	53.4	3,160.0	8.4	3,080.0	8.2	1,850.0	4.9	...	...
1996	41,726.0	30,080.0	72.1	20,680.0	49.6	3,480.0	8.3	3,680.0	8.8	2,240.0	5.4	...	...
1997	45,260.0	30,860.0	68.2	20,630.0	45.6	3,290.0	7.3	4,330.0	9.6	2,610.0	5.8	...	...
1998	45,462.8	28,227.9	62.1	18,508.4	40.7	2,915.2	6.4	3,400.4	7.5	3,404.0	7.5	4,355.0	9.6
1999	40,318.7	24,577.3	61.0	16,363.1	40.6	2,598.7	6.4	2,973.1	7.4	2,642.5	6.6	3,240.6	8.0
2000	40,714.8	22,884.3	56.2	15,500.0	38.1	2,296.3	5.6	2,915.9	7.2	2,172.2	5.3	4,848.0	11.9
2001	46,877.6	26,189.2	55.9	16,717.3	35.7	2,979.9	6.4	4,348.4	9.3	2,143.6	4.6	6,820.3	14.5
2002	52,743.0	28,358.9	53.8	17,860.9	33.9	3,970.6	7.5	4,190.1	7.9	2,337.2	4.4	8,654.8	16.4

Source: Hong Kong Monetary Authority.
[1]Offshore centers include the Virgin Islands, the Cayman Islands, Bermuda, and Samoa.

standards and practices in these areas, especially as Hong Kong SAR-based financial institutions conduct more investment banking activities with the mainland, where such standards remain below global standards in some respects.[8] Many observers anticipate that global investors, through their Hong Kong-based partners, will pressure mainland firms to improve their corporate accounting and governance practices.

Hub Linking Mainland with Rest of World

Hong Kong SAR has been the most important source of international funds for the mainland through a wide spectrum of external channels, including foreign direct investment (FDI), equity financing, debt issuance, and bank lending.

- Cumulative FDI from Hong Kong SAR to the mainland was estimated at about US$205 billion in 2002, or about 46 percent of China's total FDI.[9] Although the share of FDI flows from Hong Kong SAR has decreased recently, it still accounted for 34 percent of total FDI flows to the mainland in 2002 (Table 7.5);

- All but two of the 75 Chinese state-owned enterprises listed abroad at the end of 2002 were listed in Hong Kong SAR, where they had raised a cumulative sum of US$18.2 billion (Table 7.6).[10] In 2000, China-related companies (both red chips and H-shares) raised a record US$44 billion on the Hong Kong SAR market;

- China has raised more than US$4 billion in the Hong Kong SAR bond market (out of US$14 billion placed outside the mainland) over the last 10 years. Four mainland sovereign bonds were issued in Hong Kong SAR, and five mainland issues of nongovernment bonds were listed on the Hong Kong SAR exchange at the end of 2002;

- The stock of Hong Kong SAR banks' direct lending to mainland entities totaled some HK$408 billion (US$52 billion) in 1997, or about 60 percent of total foreign bank lending to the mainland (Table 7.7).[11] Lending to the mainland by Hong Kong SAR banks has since declined, largely because of poor loan repayments;

- Hong Kong SAR banks have been active in arranging syndicated loans and floating-rate notes for use on the mainland. At the peak in

---

[8]Some proposed enhancements to Hong Kong SAR's regulatory governance (including clarifying the regulatory roles of the three-tier capital-market regulatory system and improving delisting practices), however, have not been proceeding as quickly as had been expected, resulting in recent calls for further rounds of consultation.

[9]Some of the FDI may be accounted for by "round tripping" of funds from the mainland to take advantage of the preferential treatment of foreign investors in China.

[10]A number of these are dual listings (also in New York).

[11]Hong Kong SAR banks' direct exposure to the mainland is relatively small, amounting to around 2 percent of total assets of the banking sector, although their indirect exposure is likely to be higher, since a portion of loans booked for use in Hong Kong SAR is used by the borrowers for their mainland operations.

Table 7.6. Hong Kong SAR H-Shares: Listings and Funds Raised

Period	Main Board		Growth Enterprise Market Board		Total		
	New listings (number)	Funds raised (million U.S. dollars)	New listings (number)	Funds raised (million U.S. dollars)	New listings (number)	Funds raised (million U.S. dollars)	Cumulative funds raised (million U.S. dollars)
1993	6	1,052	...	.....	6	1,052	1,052
1994	9	1,278	...	...	9	1,278	2,330
1995	2	260	...	...	2	260	2,590
1996	6	884	...	...	6	884	3,474
1997	16	4,138	...	...	16	4,138	7,612
1998	2	268	...	...	2	268	7,880
1999	3	547	...	...	3	547	8,427
2000	3	6,635	3	83	6	6,718	15,145
2001	3	714	5	98	8	812	15,957
2002	4	2,164	12	136	16	2,300	18,257

Source: Hong Kong SAR authorities.

1997, syndicated loans to the mainland arranged by Hong Kong SAR banks totaled US$6.1 billion (Table 7.8).[12]

---

[12]There are two principal reasons for the dramatic decline since 1997 of syndicated loans to the mainland arranged by banks in Hong Kong SAR. First, Hong Kong SAR banks have tightened their lending requirements to mainland companies since the failure of the Chinese state investment firm Guangdong International Trust and Investment Corporation in 1998. Second, with low interest rates and high levels of liquidity on the mainland in recent years, mainland companies have had less incentive to borrow from banks in Hong Kong SAR.

China has become more integrated financially with the global economy, in tandem with its rising trade integration following its accession to the World Trade Organization (WTO) in November 2001. However, changes in China's financial sector since then have raised questions about whether Hong Kong SAR's role as a financial hub linking the mainland and the rest of the world would be eroded.

Restrictions by the government of Taiwan Province of China on Taiwanese direct investment on the mainland were relaxed in October 2002, which removed the need for the long-standing practice of routing Taiwanese investment to the mainland

Table 7.7. Banking Relations Between Hong Kong SAR and Mainland China
(In billions of Hong Kong dollars)

As of the End of:	Liabilities to China									Claims on China								
	Banks			Nonbanks			Total			Banks			Nonbanks			Total		
	HK$	F.C.	Subtotal	HK$	F.C.	Subtotal	HK$	F.C.	Subtotal	HK$	F.C.	Subtotal	HK$	F.C.	Subtotal	HK$	F.C.	Subtotal
1994	99.4	126.4	225.8	1.4	6.5	7.9	100.8	132.9	233.7	47.6	129.0	176.6	1.9	59.7	61.6	49.5	188.7	238.2
1995	110.9	105.6	216.5	2.8	6.5	9.3	113.7	112.1	225.8	52.2	171.6	223.8	2.4	62.6	65.0	54.6	234.2	288.8
1996	123.7	162.8	286.5	3.0	8.6	11.6	126.7	171.4	298.1	65.6	221.8	287.4	3.4	67.3	70.7	69.0	289.1	358.1
1997	130.9	158.9	289.8	8.6	7.9	16.5	139.5	166.8	306.3	75.5	261.7	337.2	4.0	66.9	70.9	79.5	328.6	408.1
1998	139.6	133.0	272.6	8.2	9.8	18.0	147.8	142.8	290.6	77.9	195.9	273.8	3.4	47.3	50.7	81.3	243.2	324.5
1999	106.1	129.4	235.5	10.8	15.9	26.7	116.9	145.3	262.2	50.0	156.8	206.8	2.7	36.0	38.7	52.7	192.8	245.5
2000	157.3	174.0	331.3	24.6	36.8	61.4	181.9	210.8	392.7	42.6	147.3	189.9	2.9	28.1	31.0	45.5	175.4	220.9
2001	96.0	185.0	281.0	19.4	33.8	53.2	115.4	218.8	334.2	18.5	153.7	172.2	3.2	23.0	26.2	21.7	176.7	198.4
2002	73.6	157.4	231.0	20.6	37.3	57.9	94.2	194.7	288.9	20.6	84.1	104.7	3.8	18.7	22.5	24.4	102.8	127.2

Source: Hong Kong Monetary Authority.
Notes: HK$ denotes Hong Kong dollars; F.C. denotes foreign currency.

Table 7.8. Volume of Syndicated Loans and Floating-Rate Notes Arranged by Banks in Hong Kong SAR for Use in Mainland China

	Loans		Floating-Rate Notes	
	Value (million U.S. dollars)	Growth (year on year)	Value (million U.S. dollars)	Growth (year on year)
1993	1,780	...	620	...
1994	4,236	138.0	424	−31.6
1995	5,168	22.0	155	−63.4
1996	5,857	13.3	307	98.1
1997	6,073	3.7	1,560	408.1
1998	5,522	−9.1	30	−98.1
1999	2,147	−61.1	420	1,300.0
2000	1,336	−37.8	200	−52.4
2001	828	−38.0	0	−100.0
2002	1,591	92.1	0	...

Source: Thomson Financial.

through a third party, notably Hong Kong SAR. Indeed, since July 2002, direct remittances have been permitted between mainland banks and those in Taiwan Province of China, which has reduced the intermediary role of Hong Kong SAR banks. However, Taiwanese enterprises have been using Hong Kong SAR as a funds-management center to support their manufacturing activities in the Pearl River delta, owing to Hong Kong SAR's proximity. Among these Taiwanese enterprises, 79 percent indicated that they would continue to do this even when direct economic links across the Taiwan Strait are eventually established.[13]

At the same time, China's accession to the WTO has allowed foreign banks to benefit from permission to conduct foreign-currency transactions with all types of clients, including mainland individuals and enterprises. As the second-largest foreign banking group on the mainland, Hong Kong banks will likely be the main beneficiary from the relaxation of such rules. It is expected that 10 to 20 percent of all renminbi deposits (totaling more than 10 trillion yuan) will be shifted from local to foreign banks because of the latter's better reputation, level of services, and perceived soundness. Moreover, the signing of the Closer Economic Partnership Arrangement in June 2003 between China and Hong Kong SAR reduced the asset requirement for opening branch offices to US$6 billion from US$20 billion, which would allow more of Hong Kong SAR's smaller banks to participate in the mainland banking market.

To boost the professionalism of investors in the mainland securities markets, qualified foreign institutional investors (QFIIs) were given access to mainland equity and debt markets in November 2002.[14] Participation is open to foreign funds management, insurance, securities, and banking institutions and is explicitly aimed at more established players. The QFIIs are not likely to pose a significant threat to Hong Kong SAR's status as China's preferred offshore direct financing center in the near term. With the relatively uneven quality of accounting and disclosure practices among mainland-listed companies, their high valuations and restrictive holding-period requirements are likely to limit foreign investor interest and resource commitments. Even as the QFII program becomes established, portfolio investment is likely to remain limited in the absence of liberalization of capital flows, and to be placed through the mainland companies listed on the Hong Kong SAR and other foreign stock exchanges.

Furthermore, the potential implementation of the qualified domestic institutional investors (QDIIs) scheme by China is expected to bring mutual benefits to the financial markets of Hong Kong SAR and the mainland. This scheme was proposed by the Hong Kong SAR government in 2001 and remains under active consideration by the mainland authorities. It would allow qualified mainland institutional investors to purchase foreign securities, including in Hong Kong SAR. If implemented, the QDIIs scheme

---

[13]This figure is from a survey done by the Hong Kong Trade Development Council in mid-2002.

[14]Investors would have access to all domestic-currency assets listed on domestic exchanges, including equities, government bonds, and commercial bonds and paper.

will widen the investor base of Hong Kong SAR financial markets and attract more high-quality mainland companies to list in Hong Kong SAR, thereby strengthening Hong Kong SAR's status as an international financial center.

Increasing cross-border activities are expected to present new challenges to financial market regulators and supervisors. Increasing integration with the mainland implies that Hong Kong SAR-based banks and securities firms would increasingly expand into the mainland, and vice versa. A major regulatory challenge will be to harmonize the laws, rules, and practices pertaining to banks and securities firms operating in Hong Kong SAR and on the mainland. Otherwise, regulatory arbitrage could lead to increasing risks and potential instability. Supervisory monitoring of Hong Kong SAR banks' risk taking will be made more difficult by the sometimes highly complex ownership and organizational structures of borrowing companies, which have links to both Hong Kong SAR and the mainland. Financial institutions and supervisors would therefore require increased transparency and disclosure to fully assess the legal and financial status of borrowers and other counterparties.

On balance, accelerated reforms and the opening up of China's financial sector should increase Hong Kong SAR's value as a financial hub and intermediary. Hong Kong SAR's advantages as an established international financial center would continue to attract foreign investors. To be sure, some large financial institutions may have relocated part of their back-office supporting activities, such as data processing and accounting services, to the mainland to take advantage of the lower costs and growing pool of skilled labor. Such shifts may result in some pressure on employment in Hong Kong SAR in the near future, but could also give added impetus to the ongoing structural change that is moving Hong Kong SAR toward an economy of high-value-added services.

References

Abraham, Jesse M., and Patric H. Hendershott, 1996, "Bubbles in Metropolitan Housing Markets," *Journal of Housing Research,* Vol. 7, No. 2, pp. 191–207.

Acemoglu, Daron, 2003, "Patterns of Skill Premia," *Review of Economic Studies*, Vol. 70 (April), pp. 199–230.

Advisory Committee on New Broad-Based Taxes, 2002, *Final Report to the Financial Secretary* (Hong Kong SAR).

Aziz, Jahangir, Peter Breuer, Tutaka Nishigaki, and Peter Sturm, 2000, "A Note on the Impact of China's Accession to the WTO on Hong Kong SAR," in *People's Republic of China—Hong Kong SAR, Selected Issues and Statistical Appendix*, IMF Staff Country Report No. 00/30 (Washington: International Monetary Fund).

Becker, Torbjörn, 1999, "Common Trends and Structural Change: A Dynamic Macro Model for the Pre- and Postrevolution Islamic Republic of Iran," IMF Working Paper 99/82 (Washington: International Monetary Fund).

Bernanke, Ben, Mark Gertler, and Simon Gilchrist, 1999, "The Financial Accelerator in a Quantitative Business Cycle Framework," in *Handbook of Macroeconomics*, Vol. 1C, ed. by J. B. Taylor and M. Woodford (New York: North Holland–Elsevier Science).

Blanchard, Olivier-Jean, 1981, "Output, the Stock Market, and Interest Rates," *American Economic Review,* Vol. 71 (March), pp. 132–43.

Bray, Mark, ed., 1993, "The Economics and Financing of Education: Hong Kong SAR and Comparative Perspectives," Education Paper No. 20 (Hong Kong SAR: University of Hong Kong, Faculty of Education).

Cassola, Nuno, and Claudio Morana, 2002, "Monetary Policy and the Stock Market in the Euro Area," ECB Working Paper No. 119 (Frankfurt: European Central Bank).

Cheng, Yuk-Shing, Weiguo Lu, and Christopher Findlay, 1998, "Hong Kong's Economic Relationship with China," *Journal of the Asia Pacific Economy*, Vol. 3, No. 1, pp. 104–30.

China, People's Republic of, Ministry of Communication, 1999, "China Water Transportation Development Report" (Beijing).

China Foreign Trade Statistical Yearbook, 1999 (Beijing).

China Statistics Press, 2001, *China Statistical Yearbook 2000*, 21st ed. (Beijing).

CLSA Emerging Markets, 2001, "Hong Kong Market Strategy—Hong Kong's Future: Tough Choice to Stay Afloat" (November).

Davis, Donald R., 1998, "Technology, Unemployment, and Relative Wages in a Global Economy," *European Economic Review,* Vol. 42 (November), pp. 1613–33.

Deininger, Klaus W., and Lyn Squire, 1996, "A New Data Set Measuring Income Inequality," *World Bank Economic Review,* Vol. 10 (September), pp. 565–91.

Feenstra, Robert C., and Gordon H. Hanson, 1996, "Globalization, Outsourcing and Wage Inequality," *American Economic Review*, Vol. 86 (May), pp. 240–45.

———, 2001, "Intermediaries in Entrepôt Trade: Hong Kong Re-exports of Chinese Goods," NBER Working Paper No. 8088 (Cambridge, Massachusetts: National Bureau of Economic Research).

Freeman, Richard B., and Lawrence F. Katz, 1994, "Rising Wage Inequality: The United States v. Other Advanced Countries," in *Working Under Different Rules*, ed. by Richard B. Freeman (New York: Russell Sage Foundation), pp. 29–62.

Gerlach, Stefan, and Wensheng Peng, 2002, "Bank Lending and Property Prices in Hong Kong," *Hong Kong Monetary Authority Quarterly Bulletin* (August), pp. 1–10.

Harvard Consultancy Team, 1999, "Improving Hong Kong's Health Care System: Why and for Whom?" (Hong Kong SAR, Health and Welfare Bureau).

Hong Kong Monetary Authority (HKMA), 2001, *Research Memoranda* (November).

Hong Kong SAR, Task Force on the Review of Civil Service Pay Policy and System, 2002, *Phase One Final Report* (Hong Kong SAR).

Hong Kong SAR, Task Force on Review of Public Finances, 2002, *Final Report to the Financial Secretary* (Hong Kong SAR).

Hong Kong SAR Census and Statistics Department, 1997–2001 "Survey of Regional Representation by Overseas Companies in Hong Kong" (Hong Kong SAR).

Hong Kong SAR General Chamber of Commerce, 2000, "China's Entry into the WTO and the Impact on Hong Kong Business" (June).

Hong Kong SAR Government, 2002, *Hong Kong SAR Yearbook 2001* (Hong Kong SAR: Government Printer).

———, 2003, *Report on Manpower Projection to 2007* (Hong Kong SAR: Government Printer).

Hong Kong SAR Trade Development Council, 2000, "Hong Kong as a Sourcing Center for China-Made Products" (February).

———, 2001a, "China's WTO Accession and Implications for Hong Kong" (November).

———, 2001b, "Profiles of Hong Kong Major Service Industries."

———, 2002, "Hong Kong's Trade and Trade Supporting Services: New Developments and Prospects" (January).

Hong Kong and Shanghai Banking Corporation (HSBC), 2002, "Hong Kong Property: Things Can Only Get Better: Housing Market Is the Emergency Exit" (August 30).

Hsieh, Chang-Tai, and Keong T. Woo, 2000, "The Impact of Outsourcing to China on Hong Kong's Labor Market" (unpublished; Princeton, New Jersey: Princeton University).

International Monetary Fund (IMF), 2000 and 2001, "Hong Kong SAR Staff Report and Selected Issues Paper" (Washington).

———, 2002, "People's Republic of China—Hong Kong SAR—Selected Issues and Statistical Appendix," IMF Country Report No. 02/99 (Washington).

———, 2003, "People's Republic of China—Hong Kong Special Administrative Region: Financial System Stability Assessment," IMF Country Report No. 03/191 (Washington).

Jiang, Guorong, Nancy Tang, and Eve Law, 2001, "Cost-Benefit Analysis of Developing Debt Markets," *Hong Kong Monetary Authority Quarterly Bulletin* (November), pp. 1–18.

Kalra, Sanjay, Dubravko Mihaljek, and Christoph Duenwald, 2000, "Property Prices and Speculative Bubbles: Evidence from Hong Kong SAR," IMF Working Paper 00/2 (Washington: International Monetary Fund).

King, Robert, Charles Plosser, James Stock, and Mark Watson, 1991, "Stochastic Trends and Economic Fluctuation," *American Economic Review,* Vol. 81, pp. 819–40.

Kiyotaki, Nobuhiro, and John Moore, 1997, "Credit Cycles," *Journal of Political Economy,* Vol. 105 (April), pp. 211–48.

Liu, H. K., 1997, *Income Inequality and Economic Development* (Hong Kong: City University of Hong Kong Press).

Morgan Stanley, 2002, "Where Are the Risks?" *Hong Kong Financial Services* (October 8).

Organization for Economic Cooperation and Development (OECD), 2002a, *Education at a Glance—OECD Indicators* (Paris).

———, 2002b, *Highlights of Public Sector Pay and Employment Trends: 2002 Update* (Paris).

Peng, Wensheng, 2002, "What Drives Property Prices in Hong Kong?" *Hong Kong Monetary Authority Quarterly Bulletin* (August), pp. 19–33.

———, Lillian Cheung, and Kelvin Fan, 2001, "Sources of Unemployment: Recent Developments and Prospects," *Hong Kong Monetary Authority Quarterly Bulletin* (November), pp. 33–48.

Peng, Wensheng, Lillian Cheung, and Cynthia Leung, 2001, "The Property Market and the Macro-Economy," *Hong Kong Monetary Authority Quarterly Bulletin* (May), pp. 40–49.

Prasad, Eswar S., 2002, "Wage Inequality in the United Kingdom, 1975–99," *Staff Papers*, International Monetary Fund, Vol. 49, No. 3, pp. 339–63.

———, 2004, "The Unbearable Stability of the German Wage Structure: Evidence and Interpretation," *Staff Papers*, International Monetary Fund, Vol. 51, forthcoming.

Rumbaugh, Thomas, and Nicholas Blancher, 2004, "China: International Trade and WTO Accession," forthcoming in the IMF's Working Paper series.

Suen, Wing, 1995, "Sectoral Shifts: Impact on Hong Kong Workers," *Journal of International Trade and Economic Development*, Vol. 4 (July), pp. 135–52.

Wolff, Edward N., 2000, "Trade and Inequality: A Review of the Literature," U.S. Trade Deficit Review Commission.

World Bank, 1997, *China 2020: Development Challenges in the New Century* (Washington).

Recent Occasional Papers of the International Monetary Fund

226. Hong Kong SAR: Meeting the Challenges of Integration with the Mainland, edited by Eswar Prasad, with contributions from Jorge Chan-Lau, Dora Iakova, William Lee, Hong Liang, Ida Liu, Papa N'Diaye, and Tao Wang. 2004.

225. Rules-Based Fiscal Policy in France, Germany, Italy, and Spain, by Teresa Dabán, Enrica Detragiache, Gabriel di Bella, Gian Maria Milesi-Ferretti, and Steven Symansky. 2003.

224. Managing Systemic Banking Crises, by a staff team led by David S. Hoelscher and Marc Quintyn. 2003.

223. Monetary Union Among Member Countries of the Gulf Cooperation Council, by a staff team led by Ugo Fasano. 2003.

222. Informal Funds Transfer Systems: An Analysis of the Informal Hawala System, by Mohammed El Qorchi, Samuel Munzele Maimbo, and John F. Wilson. 2003.

221. Deflation: Determinants, Risks, and Policy Options, by Manmohan S. Kumar. 2003.

220. Effects of Financial Globalization on Developing Countries: Some Empirical Evidence, by Eswar S. Prasad, Kenneth Rogoff, Shang-Jin Wei, and M. Ayhan Kose. 2003.

219. Economic Policy in a Highly Dollarized Economy: The Case of Cambodia, by Mario de Zamaroczy and Sopanha Sa. 2003.

218. Fiscal Vulnerability and Financial Crises in Emerging Market Economies, by Richard Hemming, Michael Kell, and Axel Schimmelpfennig. 2003.

217. Managing Financial Crises: Recent Experience and Lessons for Latin America, edited by Charles Collyns and G. Russell Kincaid. 2003.

216. Is the PRGF Living Up to Expectations?—An Assessment of Program Design, by Sanjeev Gupta, Mark Plant, Benedict Clements, Thomas Dorsey, Emanuele Baldacci, Gabriela Inchauste, Shamsuddin Tareq, and Nita Thacker. 2002.

215. Improving Large Taxpayers' Compliance: A Review of Country Experience, by Katherine Baer. 2002.

214. Advanced Country Experiences with Capital Account Liberalization, by Age Bakker and Bryan Chapple. 2002.

213. The Baltic Countries: Medium-Term Fiscal Issues Related to EU and NATO Accession, by Johannes Mueller, Christian Beddies, Robert Burgess, Vitali Kramarenko, and Joannes Mongardini. 2002.

212. Financial Soundness Indicators: Analytical Aspects and Country Practices, by V. Sundararajan, Charles Enoch, Armida San José, Paul Hilbers, Russell Krueger, Marina Moretti, and Graham Slack. 2002.

211. Capital Account Liberalization and Financial Sector Stability, by a staff team led by Shogo Ishii and Karl Habermeier. 2002.

210. IMF-Supported Programs in Capital Account Crises, by Atish Ghosh, Timothy Lane, Marianne Schulze-Ghattas, Aleš Bulíř, Javier Hamann, and Alex Mourmouras. 2002.

209. Methodology for Current Account and Exchange Rate Assessments, by Peter Isard, Hamid Faruqee, G. Russell Kincaid, and Martin Fetherston. 2001.

208. Yemen in the 1990s: From Unification to Economic Reform, by Klaus Enders, Sherwyn Williams, Nada Choueiri, Yuri Sobolev, and Jan Walliser. 2001.

207. Malaysia: From Crisis to Recovery, by Kanitta Meesook, Il Houng Lee, Olin Liu, Yougesh Khatri, Natalia Tamirisa, Michael Moore, and Mark H. Krysl. 2001.

206. The Dominican Republic: Stabilization, Structural Reform, and Economic Growth, by a staff team led by Philip Young, comprising Alessandro Giustiniani, Werner C. Keller, Randa E. Sab, and others. 2001.

205. Stabilization and Savings Funds for Nonrenewable Resources, by Jeffrey Davis, Rolando Ossowski, James Daniel, and Steven Barnett. 2001.

204. Monetary Union in West Africa (ECOWAS): Is It Desirable and How Could It Be Achieved? by Paul Masson and Catherine Pattillo. 2001.

203. Modern Banking and OTC Derivatives Markets: The Transformation of Global Finance and Its Implications for Systemic Risk, by Garry J. Schinasi, R. Sean Craig, Burkhard Drees, and Charles Kramer. 2000.

202. Adopting Inflation Targeting: Practical Issues for Emerging Market Countries, by Andrea Schaechter, Mark R. Stone, and Mark Zelmer. 2000.

201. Developments and Challenges in the Caribbean Region, by Samuel Itam, Simon Cueva, Erik Lundback, Janet Stotsky, and Stephen Tokarick. 2000.

200. Pension Reform in the Baltics: Issues and Prospects, by Jerald Schiff, Niko Hobdari, Axel Schimmelpfennig, and Roman Zytek. 2000.

199. Ghana: Economic Development in a Democratic Environment, by Sérgio Pereira Leite, Anthony Pellechio, Luisa Zanforlin, Girma Begashaw, Stefania Fabrizio, and Joachim Harnack. 2000.

198. Setting Up Treasuries in the Baltics, Russia, and Other Countries of the Former Soviet Union: An Assessment of IMF Technical Assistance, by Barry H. Potter and Jack Diamond. 2000.

197. Deposit Insurance: Actual and Good Practices, by Gillian G.H. Garcia. 2000.

196. Trade and Trade Policies in Eastern and Southern Africa, by a staff team led by Arvind Subramanian, with Enrique Gelbard, Richard Harmsen, Katrin Elborgh-Woytek, and Piroska Nagy. 2000.

195. The Eastern Caribbean Currency Union—Institutions, Performance, and Policy Issues, by Frits van Beek, José Roberto Rosales, Mayra Zermeño, Ruby Randall, and Jorge Shepherd. 2000.

194. Fiscal and Macroeconomic Impact of Privatization, by Jeffrey Davis, Rolando Ossowski, Thomas Richardson, and Steven Barnett. 2000.

193. Exchange Rate Regimes in an Increasingly Integrated World Economy, by Michael Mussa, Paul Masson, Alexander Swoboda, Esteban Jadresic, Paolo Mauro, and Andy Berg. 2000.

192. Macroprudential Indicators of Financial System Soundness, by a staff team led by Owen Evans, Alfredo M. Leone, Mahinder Gill, and Paul Hilbers. 2000.

191. Social Issues in IMF-Supported Programs, by Sanjeev Gupta, Louis Dicks-Mireaux, Ritha Khemani, Calvin McDonald, and Marijn Verhoeven. 2000.

190. Capital Controls: Country Experiences with Their Use and Liberalization, by Akira Ariyoshi, Karl Habermeier, Bernard Laurens, Inci Ötker-Robe, Jorge Iván Canales Kriljenko, and Andrei Kirilenko. 2000.

189. Current Account and External Sustainability in the Baltics, Russia, and Other Countries of the Former Soviet Union, by Donal McGettigan. 2000.

188. Financial Sector Crisis and Restructuring: Lessons from Asia, by Carl-Johan Lindgren, Tomás J.T. Baliño, Charles Enoch, Anne-Marie Gulde, Marc Quintyn, and Leslie Teo. 1999.

187. Philippines: Toward Sustainable and Rapid Growth, Recent Developments and the Agenda Ahead, by Markus Rodlauer, Prakash Loungani, Vivek Arora, Charalambos Christofides, Enrique G. De la Piedra, Piyabha Kongsamut, Kristina Kostial, Victoria Summers, and Athanasios Vamvakidis. 2000.

186. Anticipating Balance of Payments Crises: The Role of Early Warning Systems, by Andrew Berg, Eduardo Borensztein, Gian Maria Milesi-Ferretti, and Catherine Pattillo. 1999.

185. Oman Beyond the Oil Horizon: Policies Toward Sustainable Growth, edited by Ahsan Mansur and Volker Treichel. 1999.

184. Growth Experience in Transition Countries, 1990–98, by Oleh Havrylyshyn, Thomas Wolf, Julian Berengaut, Marta Castello-Branco, Ron van Rooden, and Valerie Mercer-Blackman. 1999.

183. Economic Reforms in Kazakhstan, Kyrgyz Republic, Tajikistan, Turkmenistan, and Uzbekistan, by Emine Gürgen, Harry Snoek, Jon Craig, Jimmy McHugh, Ivailo Izvorski, and Ron van Rooden. 1999.

182. Tax Reform in the Baltics, Russia, and Other Countries of the Former Soviet Union, by a staff team led by Liam Ebrill and Oleh Havrylyshyn. 1999.

181. The Netherlands: Transforming a Market Economy, by C. Maxwell Watson, Bas B. Bakker, Jan Kees Martijn, and Ioannis Halikias. 1999.

180. Revenue Implications of Trade Liberalization, by Liam Ebrill, Janet Stotsky, and Reint Gropp. 1999.

179. Disinflation in Transition: 1993–97, by Carlo Cottarelli and Peter Doyle. 1999.

178. IMF-Supported Programs in Indonesia, Korea, and Thailand: A Preliminary Assessment, by Timothy Lane, Atish Ghosh, Javier Hamann, Steven Phillips, Marianne Schulze-Ghattas, and Tsidi Tsikata. 1999.

177. Perspectives on Regional Unemployment in Europe, by Paolo Mauro, Eswar Prasad, and Antonio Spilimbergo. 1999.

Note: For information on the titles and availability of Occasional Papers not listed, please consult the IMF's *Publications Catalog* or contact IMF Publications Services.